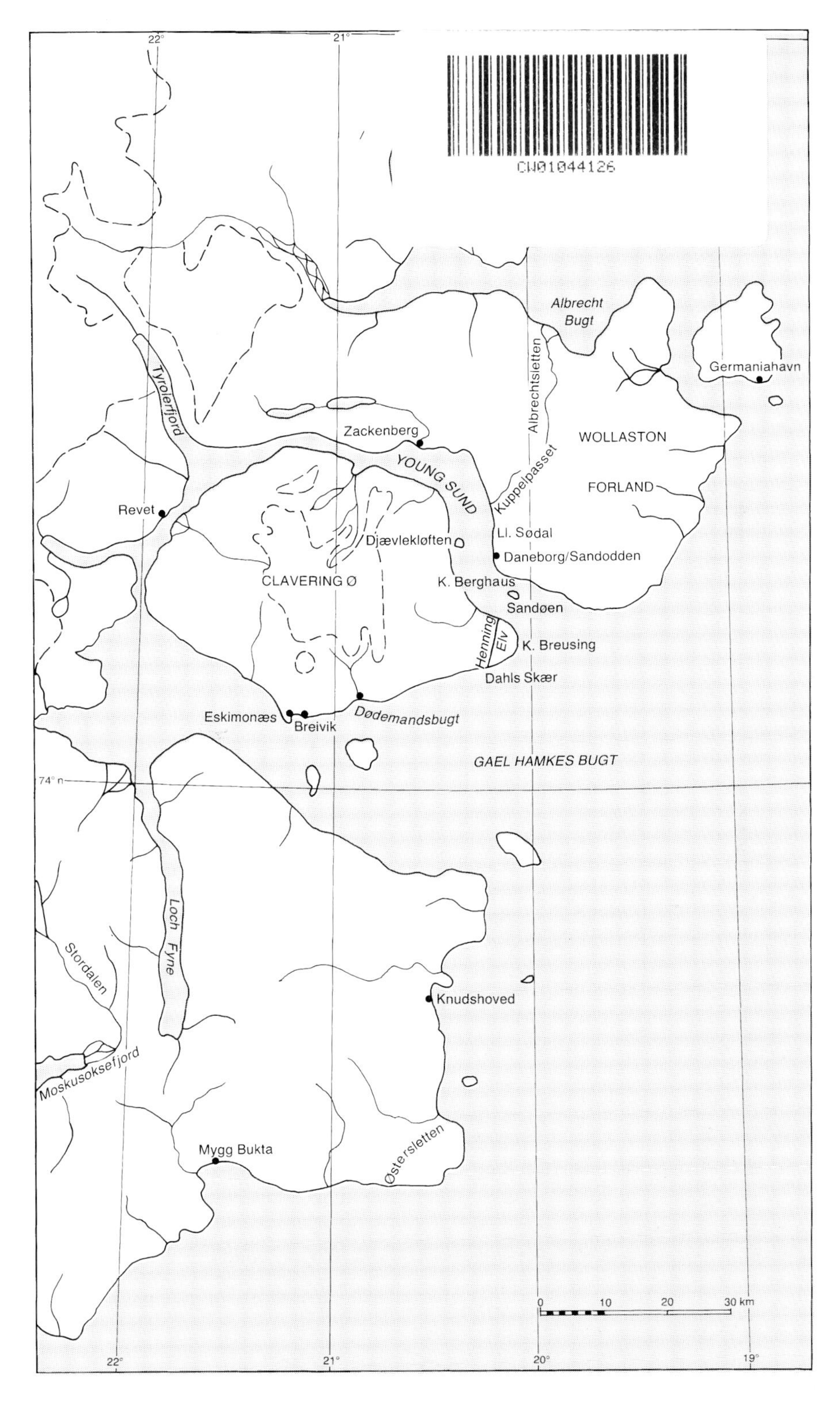

MAP 2: DETAIL OF THE AREA AROUND DANEBORG

Peter Schmidt Mikkelsen

ONE THOUSAND DAYS WITH SIRIUS

THE GREENLAND SLEDGE PATROL

Translated from the Danish original

by

David Matthews
and
Peter Schmidt Mikkelsen

ONE THOUSAND DAYS WITH SIRIUS

THE GREENLAND SLEDGE PATROL

First published in 1986 in Danish as
Tusind dage med Sirius
by Gyldendal

ISBN: 0-9950773-0-3

Published by
The Steading Workshop,
Drummore of Cantray, Cawdor IV12 5XT

www.tswpublishing.co.uk

Printed by Culross, Coupar Angus, Perthshire, Scotland

Dedicated to the memory of my father,

Niels Mikkelsen

Acknowledgements

The author wishes to express his sincere gratitude to everyone who helped with the writing and preparation of the original book and to David Matthews for his excellent translation and for proactive teamwork during the preparation of this new edition.

Furthermore, he wishes to thank his old sledging partner, Claus 'Tavsur' Birkbøll, and the entire 1978-1979 Sirius team for their enduring and outstanding friendship.

Most of all, thanks to my family, Ulla, Lisa Maria and Niels, for all their patience and love.

Peter Schmidt Mikkelsen

Rønde, February 2003

The translator offers thanks to Kristin Andrews-Speed, Sue Fenton and to his daughter, Kirsten, for help with critical reading and discussion of the draft translation, and to his son, Rob, for patient assistance with the relevant computing and internet techniques.

David Matthews

Cawdor, July 2005

Contents

Plate Captions

1. *(facing page 100)* The first sunrise. For three to four months, the sun hides beneath the horizon and Northeast Greenland is a twilit world. In February the stunning moment arrives when, for the first time, the sun sheds its light on the snow covered landscape. Fladedal, February 1978.

2. 'The Syndicate Man' — Jens Chr. Gotfredsen — repairing the roof of his domain, the carpenter's shop, otherwise known as The Syndicate.

(inset) According to the motto 'self-built is well-built', the Sirius men build their own dog sledges. Everything is hand-made and adjusted down to the smallest detail to suit personal preference (see also Appendix D).

3. *(upper)* At Kap Berghaus, the Twin Otter has arrived with a new group of Sirius men ready for their 26 months service. July 1978.

(lower) The sledge dog Duppen would like to play games with a bull muskox.

4. *(upper)* Daneborg, the sledge patrol's headquarters, consists of a small cluster of humble-looking wooden houses, seen here from Harefjeldet. In the background is Young Sund and Clavering Ø. August 1977.

(lower) The supply ship *Thala Dan* anchored in Young Sund one calm summer morning. For only a few weeks of the year, around the beginning of August, ships can reach Daneborg so Sirius gets its new supplies just once a year.

5. Sledge dogs from birth to carefree puppyhood; all bred at Daneborg.

6. *(upper)* Resting on the crossing of Ingolfs Fjord. The travelling conditions and the weather are good, with a temperature of minus 33°C.

(lower) Sledge dogs at work; truly magnificent draft animals well suited to their working environment.

7. Some sledge teams are transported each year to the far north of East Greenland, in an Air Force C-130 Hercules plane. Mestersvig, February 1980.

8. *(upper)* A camp beneath the edge of Spaerregletscher at the end of Dammen. Alpefjord, March 1979.

(lower) A team following old sledge tracks; a big excitement for the dogs. Kjerulf Fjord, March '79.

9. *(upper)* Northeast Greenland, an amazing country; untamed, majestic and powerful. Peaks in the Staunings Alps seen from Alpefjord, March 1979.

(lower) Whenever possible, when the going is good, we drive with the dogs in fan formation because, with the six metre length of the traces, the dogs have maximum freedom of movement and give their best performance. Dammen, March 1979.

10. *(upper)* It is going to blow up for a storm and we have put up camp. Normally, the tent would be sited in the lee of a rock or an iceberg, but here in open country we have built a wall of snow blocks to deflect the worst of the wind. The dogs have curled up with their backs to the wind and their noses tucked into their tails so that they can breathe through the fur. Klitdal, March 1979.

(lower) Along the outer coast of Liverpool Land. Time after time we have to cross large walls of sea ice broken up by the winter storms and then re-frozen. A hard days work for dogs and men, April 1979.

11. *(upper)* In the bright, but still chill midnight sun, we travel 30 km across the large expanse of Foster Bugt from Kap Mackenzie to Bontekoe Ø. Foster Bugt, May 1979.

(lower) After the storm. The snow wall gave us quite a surprise when, at the peak of the storm, it blew over on top of the tent. Luckily there were no serious consequences other than forcing us to get out quickly and rebuild it, April 1979.

12. *(left)* In deep loose snow, the dogs can work better by

following in each other's tracks, so they are hitched in tandem. Carlsbergfjord, April 1979.

(right) On many evenings, we had a muskox visitor.

13. *(left)* Like small wilderness museums, the old Northeast Greenland hunting stations can be useful for overnight stays. The stoves, like this one inside 'Ålborghus', can be capable of baking unsurpassed french bread, May 1978.

(right) "We take no notice of day or night on the boat trips. We work when it is necessary, eat when we are hungry and sleep when we are too tired to do anything else." Asger L. Nielsen is taking his breakfast on *Britt*'s deck, July 1979.

14. *(upper)* Blomsterbugt hut has had a polar bear visit, and a good few hours repair work await the Sirius men. Kejser Franz Joseph Fjord, May 1979.

(lower) The aftermath.

15. *(upper)* Walrus sunbathing on an ice-floe; summer time.

(lower) The crew of the *Britt* are visiting a hunter's hut. The hut has been patched with tarred paper where needed, and provisions have been brought ashore. The dog food is in the wire cage (on the right) for safety against polar bear attacks. Geologfjord, July 1979.

16. *(facing page 101)* A Greenland dawn. Nordfjord, February 1979.

Preface

In 1950, the Danish government decided to establish a military dog sledge patrol in Northeast Greenland. Due to the Cold War situation at that time, the existence of this special task force was kept top secret and, to the military authorities, the patrol went by the code name 'Operation Resolut'.

In 1953, the existence of the patrol was made known to the public, and at the same time, it was given the name Sirius after the brightest star in the constellation of Canis Major.

Today, half a century later, the mission of Sirius remains the same; to maintain Danish sovereignty along the uninhabited coast from Scoresby Sund in East Greenland to Thule on the north-west coast. The patrol also exercises the military surveillance and civilian police authority within this enormous area, called Nationalparken Nord og Nordøstgrønland (The National Park of North and Northeast Greenland), an area of almost one million square km; larger than the area of France and Great Britain put together.

Sirius is unique. It is the only military dog sledge patrol in the world and it operates in one of the most spectacular and remote parts of the world, Northeast Greenland, a place of incredible beauty as well as extreme climate.

The Sirius Patrol is surprisingly small. It has never numbered more than a dozen or so members in Greenland at any one time, yet the results are impressive. Up to the present day, the patrolmen and their Greenland dogs have travelled no less than 750,000 km by dog sledge, equal to roughly nineteen times around the earth!

One might assume that being a Sirius man has changed dramatically over the years in view of all the new kinds of technical equipment that have become available. Not so. In practice, the Sirius concept has remained almost unchanged throughout the fifty years of its existence, simply because it has achieved a near-perfect way of carrying out its tasks. Two men, eleven dogs and a sledge loaded with exactly what is needed to survive an arctic winter. This is low-tech, relatively inexpensive, and as safe as it can be. Of course, the Sirius men today use satellite navigation equipment and modern radio communications, not to mention modern clothing and base station conveniences, but they still navigate by means of map and compass when necessary, live and work in small self-reliant groups and travel in a way that neither pollutes nor requires extensive back-up or an elaborate support organisation. I am certain that the cold and the blizzards hit them as hard as they ever did, but to be a member of Sirius today is a timeless experience in which one uses techniques adapted and perfected over the decades to live and work in, rather than in spite of, a hostile, beautiful and unspoilt environment.

It was my privilege to serve in Sirius from 1977 to 1979. This was more than the fulfilling of a dream; it changed my life. It gave me unforgettable experiences of extreme challenges, unlimited freedom and unbreakable teamwork.

This, then, is the story of some of those experiences. It was originally published in the mid 1980s but, until now, has not been available outside Denmark.

1. SELECTION AND TRAINING

Why apply to Sirius?

Once or twice in a lifetime, one can find oneself quite unexpectedly at a significant crossroads in life. On an otherwise ordinary day in January 1976, while I was undergoing officer training, my eyes lit on a brochure about The Sirius Sledge Patrol; a chance event that was to have an enormous impact on my life.

Nowadays, when I am giving lectures about my experiences, I am often asked what kind of people apply to join the Sirius Patrol and why on earth do they do it. Are there any common reasons or motives for it? This interest and curiosity is very understandable, especially if I am giving my audience an insight into all the drawbacks and disadvantages of being a Sirius man.

Do Sirius men, therefore, come from particular social groups of people with a certain background and do they have a common motive leading them to apply for a place in the Patrol? To the first part of the question, the answer is definitely 'no'. They come from all parts of Denmark and from all levels of society. Their natures and qualifications vary greatly. They are short, tall, thin or ... not so thin. Some are talkative, some are the silent type, some witty and some without much sense of humour at all. They vary from well-dressed men of the world to youths looking like hippies or punks. Some are sons of managing directors; some are farmers' boys. There are carpenters, factory workers, electricians and students. In short, a wide range of people with one thing in common; they are normal human beings.

As for motives, these differ as widely as the people themselves, but I think the two most common themes are an urge to travel and ... chance.

What is this urge to travel? I think it comes from the desire to see what is behind the next hill; a sense of adventure and a restlessness. An urge to travel is something I shared with most of my colleagues in the Patrol and I have felt it myself for as long as I can remember. Even in my earliest childhood it grew rapidly, thanks to some of my relatives who had tried their luck in the great new countries of the west such as America and Argentina. They returned with stories and mementoes that really fired my imagination and inspired in me, a small boy eager for knowledge of the great wide world, the urge to travel and see some of this huge world for myself.

I remember also from my childhood years a television programme about some Danish soldiers who, with dogs and sledges, travelled in a snowy wilderness. Images from that programme stayed in my mind and sowed the seeds of my later interest in Greenland; a remarkable country and a part of my native Denmark.

Thinking about the other factor, chance, I fancy it has been this that has brought many to be interested in Sirius. For my part, it was the training camp brochure that seemed to ignite my urge to see something of the world. As I looked at it that day, I realised that this could be just what I wanted. I had recently finished my training as a radio technician before being newly drafted for military service (compulsory at that time) and I was about to become an officer. I had no ties or other commitments and was in good health. Altogether I was in a good position for being chosen to take a part in the patrol. Through my parents and my childhood on a farm in the western part of Denmark, I had grown up to love nature and wildlife, so Greenland had become one of the places that I longed especially to see for myself.

The more I read about it, the more the idea appealed to me and even before I had finished reading the brochure, I had made up my mind that I wanted to become a Sirius man as soon as possible. So it was pure chance that my life took this turn when it did and I think that the same goes for many of my comrades.

Selection for Sirius training

The selection of new personnel for Sirius takes place only once a year, in October and, having made my decision to try to join, the wait was hard to endure.

In the meantime, I became a sergeant stationed with a regiment at Holstebro, a city in western Denmark, and as October approached, I began to look on the notice board each day to see if there were any bulletins or instructions on how to apply.

At last, there it was: "The Sirius Sledge Patrol is looking for applications from officers and non-commissioned officers for service in Northeast Greenland." I think that a bare 30 seconds passed before I stood, somewhat out of breath, in front of my commanding officer to ask for his help in preparing my application. He was quite amused by my eagerness to be sent out into the arctic wilderness, but he was really helpful and soon the application was ready and put in the post. The reply came soon afterwards in the form of a short message telling me to report to a certain address in Copenhagen on a certain date and submit to an examination by the military psychologists. In their wisdom, these people were to decide if I was foolish enough to be sent out into the wilds or, perhaps, if I was too foolish for it. This was a start, at least, and I showed up at the appointed time and place, with a healthy degree of scepticism. I was not alone. Half a dozen other applicants were there and it became an exciting experience.

The whole time passed in what can best be described as a friendly and happy atmosphere. There were several tests which we had to undergo during the course of the day. At one point we were confronted with a series of odd-looking pictures consisting of dots and blobs of paint; the sort of thing that a child with a vivid imagination might create in expression of its childish fantasies. In response to their questions, there seemed to be no alternative but to tell the psychologists, truthfully, that these paintings looked just like butterflies and pregnant elephants and so on.

As well as personal conversation with the psychologists, there were also group tests where four or five applicants, watched by the psychologists, were set different tests with the purpose of finding out who was and who was not suitable for arctic service. The day ended and we were sent back to our regiments with a note to say that we would be informed of the results in due course.

In this first part of the selection process, I think around 20 applicants succeeded in passing through the needle's eye by showing that, according to the tests, they were sufficiently mad to be sent out into the polar wilderness. They didn't say exactly that, but in the kind letter that I received after a restless wait, I was informed that if I was still interested, I should report to another venue at a certain time on a certain day.

Of course I was interested and so I showed up on the appointed day, in good time, at the address which appeared to be in the Danish naval station at Holmen in Copenhagen. Here for the first time, I met the chief of the sledge patrol and its guiding light for many years, Commander Mogens N. Guldbrandsen.

At first sight, this commander seemed to be a rough and unkind type of person and, in his welcoming speech, he did little to change this first impression. He did nothing to put us at our ease but told us all, without beating about the bush, that in his opinion we had better think very darned carefully one more time before we came on board this ship. If any of us were suited to the job— and he was not yet too sure about that — so that we were chosen and sent to Greenland, there would be no help for any man who became tired of it all, or thought it was too cold, or who missed his mother. There would be no chance of 'taking the bus home' or of saying: "I am tired and I don't want to play any more" because, once in Greenland, it could be months before such a poor bastard could be brought home again.

To be truthful I do not remember the exact words, but the meaning, of course, was to tell those of us who were not too certain, that now was the time to think carefully.

Guldbrandsen pointed out that it would be extremely stupid to join Sirius if we had a serious girlfriend at home, since 26 months of unbroken separation had led in the past to some very negative statistics. People do change in the course of two years, especially in the Sirius environment. Guldbrandsen also told us about the practicalities of working for Sirius. Holidays; none. Free time; in effect, none. Working hours; until the job was finished. Pay; normal rates plus a small 'Greenland allowance' which would be our only compensation for any conceivable inconvenience that we might experience.

There were a lot of hard truths in that speech and what it meant for us, and it was clear that one or two heads in the group had begun to hang a little lower. For myself, I thought: "If it is really as horrible as he makes out, why the hell is he standing here himself?" It was a long time before I came to appreciate the answer to that question.

The tests lasted for two days, including medical and dental examinations. After the first day, a few applicants who had come through the psychological tests, fell by the wayside; some because of the admonitions of Guldbrandsen, whose tough words had had the desired effect, and some because the doctors had said 'no'. On the second day of the tests, each applicant was called before a large panel consisting of Guldbrandsen, officers from the three armed forces, military psychologists, doctors and dentists. This was the last assessment. Like a final exam, each applicant was called in. It was the moment of truth.

Those of us still left were nervous and excited as we went into the meeting. Again, Guldbrandsen gave us some very encouraging information; the same story once more. This was our last chance to drop out, if we wished, with our honour intact. When all of us stood firm, he remarked that it was our own fault if we regretted it later. After that he was silent and he looked at each of us in turn; for the first time he seemed to us a more pleasant man. Then he read out the names of those who had been chosen to attend the training school.

We, the chosen, stood and watched the unsuccessful candidates as they left the room with Guldbrandsen; there was no jubilation or shouting or anything because we knew that it could have been any one of us in that group. By the time Guldbrandsen returned, we had regained some of our self-confidence. He noticed this at once and barked: "I suppose you think you are already Sirius men, but you had better listen carefully. You, who stand here, have been chosen to start at the training school, but there is absolutely no guarantee that any of you will ever join Sirius. For one thing, we don't need all of you, which means that some of you must definitely be weeded out. Secondly, we only take those who we find suitable for the job and just because you have been found suitable for training doesn't mean that you will be found suitable for Sirius."

The self-confident expressions faded quickly and Guldbrandsen continued: "From this point on, everything you do either at work or in your free time, will have some significance if you are to join Sirius. If, for example, I ever get to hear that any one of you is being sulky or angry or anything like that, then it will be 'out' because we have no use for that kind of person. Any questions?"

No-one had anything to ask!

"Good; then I expect to see you all again on 4 January. Here are some papers with practical information, which you can share round," he nodded at one of us, "and you two", he looked at two others, "please put the tables and chairs to rights and clear the ashtrays and coffee cups away."

I think we must have looked a little surprised because we were officers, by God's mercy, and thought we were above such chores. Guldbrandsen noticed this. "Yes, I forgot to mention it, but that is how we do things in Sirius. You had better get used to the fact quickly; there will be no-one coming to clean up after you."

"Yes, Commander," we answered.

"You can just call me Guldbrandsen," he replied.

"Yes, Guldbrandsen."

Sirius training school

We, eight of us, stood along the ship's rail on the Copenhagen to Oslo ferry and watched the lights of Elsinore pass by.

It was 4 January 1977 and we had started at the Sirius training school that same morning. Now, we were on our way to Norway where, for the next six weeks, we would have to participate in the Norwegian army's winter warfare training course for NATO officers. First and foremost we would learn to ski, while at the same time we would be introduced to winter warfare and survival techniques.

The day had been hectic and confusing, as it always is when starting a new job. Hurrying here and there, we had been issued with equipment, papers, tickets and so on, all at such a speed that we scarcely had time to talk to one another.

Silently we stood there on the deck of the ship, each of us doubtless wondering about our future companions. Once inside and sitting around a table, the shyness disappeared and a lively conversation started. How we did differ from each other, but soon it felt as though we were the best of friends and by dinner time we were really looking forward to our time together.

The course itself was extremely interesting in every respect. After arrival at the infantry winter and weaponry training school at Elverum, about 150 km north of Oslo, we spent the next six weeks, together with participants from the USA, UK, and Holland, undergoing a really well-planned course which I remember to this day with pleasure. Patiently, our Norwegian instructors taught us how to manage our skis on day-long training exercises, interspersed with hours of instruction in survival techniques. Not only on day and night exercises did the Norwegians help us to keep our skis pointing in the right direction, they also organised weekend breaks to various wintersports localities.

It quickly became apparent that we Danes managed best in ski-training. This was not so much because of our nationality, but more because each of us was focussed on doing really well in the eyes of our instructors. We remembered all too clearly Guldbrandsen's message that: "Well, there are still a couple of you who must be dropped". A competitive spirit developed between us, though we remained friends and respected each other. We knew also that the judgement passed on us by the Norwegians would, to a large degree, depend on our good humour and helpful attitude; two characteristics which are fundamental to well-being in the Arctic under winter conditions. It is the psychological as much as the physical side of things that fit a person for becoming a Sirius man!

Much more could be said about this course but, with a complete absence of modesty, I will just relate here what was written in an internal naval bulletin, after our return to Denmark:

"A credit to the sledge patrol!

The new team, which will go to relieve the staff of the Sirius Sledge Patrol this summer, is undergoing full time, specialist training at home. The team has just returned from its obligatory course at the Norwegian army's winter-school, which they completed with honours. For the first time, no fewer than five of the team have been awarded the Norwegian army's certificate for 30 km of cross-country skiing with shooting and it needs an extremely good performance to achieve this standard. The senior Danish officer at NATO headquarters in Kolsås reported that, during his visit to the winter training school, he received many complimentary remarks about the Dane's achievements and their commitment to the tough training."

After this, we had our quarters at Holmens Kaserne at the naval HQ in Copenhagen and, even though this old building was not renowned for its comfort and cleanliness, we had a fine time in our 12 square metre, four-man room, with nothing but a pair of two-tier bunks and four lockers.

Maybe because I had grown up in the interior of the country and never had any connection with the sea or ships, I found Holmen different and interesting with its canals, ships and old buildings. From this place, Danes had set out on voyages all over the oceans of the world. Nearby, the Norwegian sealer *Magdalene*, just after the turn of the twentieth century, had been re-named *Danmark* and had sailed northwards to Greenland to explore the last unknown regions of that land. This was precisely the same northeast coast for which we were now preparing ourselves. For a landlubber, there was plenty here to see and to dream about.

Once we had returned from Norway, Guldbrandsen called us together and told us about our future training programme. We were to travel the next day to Jutland to take part in a fortnight's shooting instruction at the Oksbøl and Borris military camps. After that, we were to go to the military engineers in Farum who had another two-week's course for us in which we would be taught all we needed to know about explosives.

Once we had been given this information and heard the practical details, we were told to fetch coffee and cups. Guldbrandsen lit his pipe, leant back in his chair and asked what we thought about the Norwegian ski course. The atmosphere was comfortable and relaxed and, after we had related our experiences with enthusiasm, Guldbrandsen told us, to our great satisfaction, that he had received flattering comments on our performance and that he hoped this would continue on our next courses. He said absolutely nothing about our fitness to join Sirius.

As we dispersed from this cosy hour, we cleaned up the room without being asked; we had begun to learn how to behave!

One month later, we gathered in the same room again. One of the group was missing, but I should explain straight away that he had not been hurt in the shooting or explosives training from which we were recently returned. No; our comrade had simply, one day, told Guldbrandsen that he had come to the conclusion that Sirius was not for him. Guldbrandsen said that even though it was a bit late in the day to realise this, it was a sensible decision because, as long as we were still in Denmark, it was just a matter of saying so and he would be free of his obligations; later on, it would be an entirely different matter. For the umpteenth time, he emphasised all the things to which we would have to wave goodbye. There must be absolutely no doubt left in our minds about what would be involved in becoming a member of the Patrol in Greenland.

In the remaining part of the training time, we had regular meetings with Guldbrandsen and his assistant coordinator, sergeant-major Claus R. Birkbøll.

The tasks of the Sirius coordinators are many and varied. Besides the selection and training of new Sirius recruits, they are the official Sirius representatives within the military, with headquarters within the defence department. In peacetime, it is the Sirius coordinator who has to decide which parts of Northeast Greenland shall be patrolled from year to year and, with the aid of daily radio contact, the position of the various sledge teams is always known to him. As well as that, lists have to be compiled of all the supplies which are needed and which must be sent to Greenland once a year by ship. These supplies have to be purchased and collected together for packing in Denmark; a huge job for the coordinator.

Our meetings with Guldbrandsen and Birkbøll were, for the most part, concerned with learning specifically about Northeast Greenland, including navigational methods using map and compass. This is a little more complicated than in Denmark itself because of the large magnetic variation in an area so near to the magnetic and geographic north poles. A great deal of emphasis was placed on studying and memorising the maps and their main features, in case we should ever find ourselves without them. We were also lectured on the history of Northeast Greenland and on its wildlife and we were given maps and a long list of books that we could borrow from the library, to study — in our free time!

Besides these activities, we attended a constant stream of other courses several times each week, on subjects which included learning old Samuel Morse's ingenious language to enable us to communicate by using wireless telegraphy when out on patrol. Almost every day at some point during the rest of the training time, therefore, we sat in the naval tactical school listening to an endless stream of dots and dashes.

Someone, most probably a Sirius man, once said: "A Sirius man can do anything — except give birth!"

The last part of the sentence is undoubtedly true, since applications from women to join the patrol were not considered. As for the first part, well of course for a few of us it might be partly true but, if we persevered a little more, it might be truer (and more modest) to say: "A Sirius man should (hopefully) be able to do anything..."

The best way of living up to such a demanding requirement is, of course, to train to do just that. The next best way is to believe that one can do anything, especially if this belief can be combined with an ability to improvise and to recognise and make good use of a little bit of good luck — if that shows up.

It requires plenty of self-belief and skill at improvising, not to mention luck, to convince a boat's motor that it really can start again and that there is nothing seriously wrong with it, while drifting round in the middle of a fjord in Northeast Greenland, with the nearest service station about 1500 km away.

"It is unlikely that there will be such an unexpected and unfortunate situation," could be a suitable reply to this. Yes, of course, but the chance of it actually occurring is confirmed by theories on the laws of nature propounded by a clever man called Edsel Murphy. One of these laws, known as Murphy's Law, states something to the effect that: "If a thing can go wrong, then sooner or later it will go wrong, invariably at the most inconvenient time."

In the light of such a powerful law, which many will surely accept as proven fact, it is desirable to have, if possible, a little more than just self-confidence, improvisation and luck.

Thinking back to the example of the motor that would not start and taking into account the fact that there is no specialist mechanic in the patrol, it is easy to understand how important it is that all patrol members know the principles of how an engine works, how to tackle such an unforeseen situation and of the importance of properly maintaining equipment to try to prevent such accidents happening in the first place.

To this end, we took part in a motor mechanics' course and, even though this and the other courses gave us little more than superficial understanding of the subjects, they at least gave us some basic knowledge to underpin our competence.

Motors are one thing; animals and people are something else. Therefore our medical officer, Leif Vanggaard, taught us the most elementary principles of medicine. He placed emphasis on how to recognise the symptoms of illness, to show us that if we could not make a diagnosis, we could at least describe the symptoms accurately over the radio. Vanggaard or another doctor would then be able to decide on appropriate treatment. For such treatment, each sledge team carried a comprehensive first aid box with medicines and with equipment for dealing with accidents, fractures and so on.

Appendicitis? Yes, of course, we had to know that the appendix is located on the right ... no ... left ... oh well, now it doesn't matter so much.

In books about Greenland in the old days, one can read about the terrible sufferings that arctic travellers endured at that time and imagine that such troubles were caused by tough weather conditions or bad equipment. If the stories are to be believed, and I think most of them are, the worst problem and the one that was most feared, was toothache.

For that reason, each of us had go to the surgery of dentist Finn Prætorius who examined our teeth in minute detail and filled every actual or suspected cavity. Wisdom teeth of doubtful character he didn't care for at all, so there were a couple of us who, for a while, had to go around with swollen jaws like gorillas.

It is not hard to imagine, then, that this Sirius training school never became monotonous. No sooner had we finished one course than there was another to start; a weather course at the Meteorological Institute, a radio course, and so on. In spite of all this activity, we were still determined to go through fire and water in order to join the patrol. We were to prove this beyond doubt when we went to the Naval technical school and, dressed in asbestos suits and carrying oxygen bottles and fire extinguishers, we underwent training on how to fight fire and survive in smoke.

The Sledge Patrol only gets its supplies delivered to Greenland once a year. As well as food for men and dogs, thousands of other items have to be supplied, both large and small, which at home can so easily be bought in supermarkets and stores. All these things have to be ordered, packed and then despatched by a given date, or else be a year late arriving at their destination.

According to the maxim 'To do it properly, do it yourself', it was the applicants at training school who carried out the work of packing all the supplies as these arrived in a constant stream at the Sirius central depot which, at that time, was located in a cosy old warehouse at Holmen. There were other sound reasons for doing the packing ourselves. For one thing, we would become familiar with the types of equipment and supplies that were needed; we would also get some exercise after hours sitting on the school bench. Last but not least, if anything got broken during transport to Greenland, there would be no doubt about who was to blame! We enjoyed these hours of hard work and, at the same time, we began to see proof that the patrol really existed as we closed and wrote on each case: *To be shipped to Sirius Sledge Patrol, 3992 Daneborg, Greenland.*

After that there was little more to do than hope that one day we would have the same destination and that the same address would be put on our own bags. We still amounted to more applicants than were needed. The day for final selection was coming closer, the date had been fixed, and all of us knew what the procedure would be.

This form of selection procedure needs a little explanation so that it is not misunderstood. Firstly, the few who would eventually be selected for Sirius would have to look at each other, trust each other, and listen to each other's stupid jokes hundreds of times in the course of the next two years. There would be no possibility of escape, of changing one's company, or of having a private life. Knowing about these factors and knowing that the choice has to be made, what then is the best way of making the selection?

Of course, it could be left to a lucky draw in which everyone would have the same chance. Yet for such an important decision to be left to a lottery, might mean that someone is selected who is not so well fitted to be a part of the group.

Who, then, is the best to judge whether or not any individual is not best suited to fit into the team? There has to be one right answer, on reflection, and that is the team itself.

In the days leading up to final selection, therefore, each of us had private discussions with Guldbrandsen who would have to make the final decisions. These conversations were taken very seriously and he never once revealed his own opinions about us and our comrades. Each of us made a 'hit list' of our fellow applicants, starting with number one, the person we would most like to have as a colleague for the next two years, on to number two and so on. At the same time, we gave our reasons for making the choice and our evaluation of the characteristics of each person. This method of choosing seemed good, but it was not a pleasant task to weigh one's comrades against one another, well knowing that the loser might not achieve his ambition to join Sirius. It was a real relief when all the conversations were finished and Guldbrandsen showed up one afternoon at the packing warehouse.

Each of us knew, of course, that this was the moment of truth, but we carried on with what we were doing. Quietly, he went around saying something in a low voice to each of us in turn. For myself, I was standing at the back of the shed and could not hear what was being said to the others.

Finally, he came to me and said:

"Mikkel, are you still ready to go to Northeast Greenland?"

"Yes," I answered.

"Good, then you can reckon to be leaving on 18 July."

In this quiet way, we were given the news. There were no shouts of jubilation and it was not until he called us all together to give us some practical details that we discovered there was one missing. Shortly after Guldbrandsen left us, this one friend came round and said goodbye and good luck; then he left, looking rather sad and dejected. It was some time before the good humour returned to the rest of us but, of course, we had been selected and we were over the moon. We celebrated that evening.

It was a great relief that the tension was at last over. Up to now we had not dared to make any personal preparations or, for instance, to decide what personal possessions to pack for shipment. There were a lot of things we had to do now, fast, before leaving home and civilisation behind for two years. We would have to buy a mass of personal necessities because, of course, there are no shops in the area where Sirius operates. It was funny to watch the face of the local shopkeepers when going in and asking for 30 cartons of cigarettes, 40 boxes of pipe tobacco and 20 of pipe cleaners or, at the supermarket checkout, taking out 6 bottles of shampoo, 18 toothbrushes and 25 tubes of toothpaste, as well as a large assortment of combs, nail-clippers etc; There were not even any special sale offers tempting us to buy such quantities!

At last everything, both personal and for the patrol, was ready, packed in boxes and sent for shipment. The training school was closed and there was just one short week before departure. As there was nothing more to be done at Holmen, we had permission to take the time off, giving us the opportunity to spend these last few days with our families. Before scattering around the country, we were given the much-coveted Sirius badges to be sewn onto our uniforms. For the first time, we felt as if we were almost Sirius men.

Even though two years is not such a long time when looking back, it was an odd feeling at the time to be saying goodbye to one's relatives, knowing that it would be 26 months before we would see them again. Unbidden, it crossed one's mind that it might be for the last time for some, so many things can happen, and in those last days before departure there was a chance to talk about thoughts and feelings that are normally kept deep within oneself.

In a flash, the time for departure arrived. Standing on the railway station with rucksacks and suitcases and the train ready to leave, we embraced each other and tried to be cheerful, smiling optimistically and saying: "Have a good time and we will see you again in two years." It was a relief, in a way, to get onto the train and hear the guard's whistle blow. Worries were left behind. Now is reality; it has been no more than a dream for such a long time; Sirius and Greenland.

2. SUMMER

Arrival in East Greenland

It is 8 o'clock in the evening and we are flying high above the cold waters of the Denmark Strait on board a Twin Otter, a small twin-engined plane chartered from the Icelandic company *Flugfélag Nordurlands*. In the pilot's seat is one of the owners, Sigurdur Adalsteinsson, whose cool head and skill as a pilot are legendary in East Greenland. In the brilliant arctic sunshine, we are northbound from Keflavik where we arrived earlier in the day by scheduled flight from Kastrup, the international airport at Copenhagen. On this flight we will land at Mestersvig to re-fuel, before continuing further north to Daneborg, the sledge patrol's headquarters and our home for the next two years. For the moment that lies ahead and right now, we have our noses glued to the cabin windows.

It is an almost indescribable prospect. Far below, the sun reflects off the water which seems to be littered with an enormous number of small white pieces of mosaic. This is the east Greenland pack ice, consisting of an incalculably large number of icefloes which together form a perpetually moving mass; the Storis (great ice). This formidable barrier cuts off the sea route to Northeast Greenland for all except a few weeks in each summer.

Most fascinating to us though, in these moments, is the land which slowly and majestically rises above the horizon, first as a thin line of shadow but soon revealing itself to our eyes as a fantastic panorama of dark blue and blinding white. Mountain peak after mountain peak rears up and, between the peaks, we can glimpse the eternal snows of the inland ice-cap, smooth and untrodden. We are approaching the Blosseville Coast. Conversations in the plane become muted; we are overwhelmed by the wildness and the beauty of it all.

Still at a high altitude, we pass the mouth of Scoresby Sund, the largest fjord system in the world. On its north side, we can just see some irregularities in the landscape beneath us; the Scoresby Sund colony where about 500 inhabitants live in the most northerly Greenlander settlement on the east coast. From here northwards, the coast is totally uninhabited all the way round to Thule on the west; the only exception being the few Danes who are stationed here and with whom we shall soon have our first meeting.

As Sigurdur begins our descent, we can see that the mountain ranges which, from high above showed only as blue and black shapes, now begin to reveal new colours. We are surprised at the variety, each mountain displaying a different combination with brown being dominant, but every conceivable shade from yellow to red to blueish violet seems to be there.

The plane banks into a turn and directly ahead of us we can see the long straight line of Mestersvig airfield. Ten minutes later and I step for the first time onto Greenland soil. It is undeniably a great moment and the sharp coolness of the air outside the plane is a surprise too, making the face and lungs tingle. It is fresh and without smell, but we have no time to reflect on these things; half a dozen people are gathered to greet us and give us a welcome. They are the airfield personnel, naturally curious to see what kind of guys are moving in. Living as they do in a remote area larger than France and Great Britain put together and inhabited by fewer than three dozen people, it is quite an event when new neighbours arrive.

Soon, we are on board the plane again and flying further north with all the seats full. Besides us new Sirius men, we have Guldbrandsen, Birkbøll and some technicians and craftsmen who will be with us just for the summer. A fair amount of space in the plane is taken up by boxes of fresh fruit, vegetables and eggs which are not everyday food in Greenland. Last, but not least, there are a couple of sacks of mail for the Sirius men at Daneborg who have been waiting a long time for news from their families and friends.

The time is already 11pm but brilliant sunshine still lights the spectacular landscape below us; we are in the land of the midnight sun where, in the summer months, the sun never sets. A couple of hours more flying and Daneborg lies down there, somewhere, but after several vain attempts at landing, it is obvious that we cannot make it. There is a layer of fog along the outer coast with long tendrils, like cotton wool, extending up the fjord systems. Even though Sigurdur circles the landing place many times looking for a small hole in the fog, instructing the Sirius people down below to fire off signal flares to mark the runway, he at last has to give up. He sets a course inland beyond the reach of the fog and after half an hour or so, we land in Stordalen beside a group of white tents which make up the summer camp for a team of geologists. Now well past midnight, it is decided we have to stay where we are until morning. Since the pilots are a long way from home, they must in any case have a few hours rest before they continue.

We new Sirius men are disappointed at the delay in getting to Daneborg; we are not yet used to the fact that, in this part of the world, few things happen according to a timetable. Although tired after the many hours of travelling and so many new experiences, we have no urge to get into our sleeping bags because it is so light. Some of us decide to take a walk and in no more than a couple of minutes, the camp is out of sight behind a small hill and the complete silence of the arctic descends on us. We don't talk, we just walk slowly, each of us lost in his own thoughts. It is scarcely believable that only 18 hours have passed since we left the noise and bustle of Denmark and now we are enveloped in the silence of a nature unchanged for thousands of years. The only sound we hear as we stop momentarily to savour the experience, comes from a small melt-stream gurgling through the stony landscape. Unbidden, we go over to it and sit for a while as the stress of the day drains away from us. Before very long, it dawns on us that we are beginning to feel cold; in spite of the sunshine, the temperature is only a degree or two above freezing. It is well into the night as we stroll back to the camp for a short sleep that we do not really want.

Later the same afternoon, we land without problems on the flat gravel at Kap Berghaus, just a few kilometres from Daneborg (plate three). All traces of the fog have entirely disappeared during the course of the morning. It is an exciting moment when, once again, we step out of the plane. Some of the folk waiting outside are those with whom, for better or worse, we shall have to spend the next 365 days, but at first sight they seem quite ordinary and normal. This half of the group, our future companions, are dressed in civilian clothes ready to fly back to Iceland for dental visits with the additional possibility of 'getting their compasses re-aligned' as one might delicately put it. They will be there for a short week before Sigurdur will fly them north again so that they can continue with their second season.

The other half of the group look in a way more suited to the landscape. They are dressed in blue naval fatigues much the same as those we newcomers have already changed into, but with the difference that ours are new and shiny whereas theirs are well-worn and faded by the sun. There are no badges of rank to be seen for the simple reason that it is Greenland experience rather than military seniority or age that count here. The new arrivals will nearly always be able to tell who has the authority and the know-how by their well-used and faded clothing. Worn clothing is not as a rule associated with laziness and is, in a way, a badge of office in the patrol.

There is another feature that characterises all the men standing there; they have the weatherbeaten and sun-tanned faces that result from long exposure to the arctic climate.

Approaching each other, we shake hands and introduce ourselves, receiving in return a welcome to Sirius. There is no time for more; the all-important mail must be retrieved and the plane unloaded, before being re-fuelled and re-loaded with the returning baggage and outgoing mail for all those at home in Denmark. Everyone works fast and soon the plane, with the second-year folk on board, is just a distant hum heading southwards.

The rest of us move on to Daneborg itself. There is no real

road, only a few rough tracks along which the waiting tractor and its trailer cabin will ferry us. Some prefer to walk and for this, change into rubber boots, since the ground is in places wet and swampy due to the summer melt-water which is unable to soak away through the permanently frozen ground.

After half an hour of walking, some radio masts appear in the distance, soon followed by some buildings. We have arrived.

Daneborg lies on the east side of Young Sund, a fjord which runs in from the outer Greenland coast between Clavering Ø and the Wollaston Forland peninsula. It was given this in preference to the original name of Sandodden. The first time that Europeans reached this area was in 1823 when the British captain Douglas Clavering, with the good ship *Griper*, reached Gael Hamkes Bay and thereby scared away the last of the Northeast Greenland eskimos (it was actually the firing of rifles that scared the native people away). Clavering only came close enough to get a glimpse into Young Sund and it was not until the arrival of the Second German North Pole Expedition under Captain Karl Koldewey, in 1869, that Young Sund was properly explored. The Germans came this way in winter time during a sledge trip from Germaniahavn where their ship *Germania* lay frozen into its winter harbour, and they reached as far as the end of Tyrolerfjord which is the continuation of Young Sund. A lot of place names, well known to most travellers in East Greenland, originated with this expedition; Zackenberg, Kap Berghaus, Kap Breusing, Kuhn Ø and Kejser Franz Joseph Fjord to name just a few.

To return to the subject of Daneborg, the East Greenland Trapping Company first built a hunting station here in 1923. This continued as an active trapper's station until 1941 and to this day the original Sandodden hut stands fully intact. Its woodwork still looks fresh; clear evidence of the astonishing durability of wood here in Northeast Greenland where the dry air means that rotting progresses only very slowly.

In Daneborg's history there was another milestone in 1947 when the Greenland Technical Organisation (GTO) erected a weather station. 1951 saw the building of the new Sirius sledge patrol headquarters which previously, in the first year of the patrol's existence, had been on Ella Ø. Today, Sirius is the only year-round activity at Daneborg since the weather station was closed down in 1975.

The community at Daneborg

Many outsiders might take it for granted that nowadays there is an all-year-round communal utility at Daneborg. This includes supplies of electricity, water and heating as well as the maintenance of buildings and equipment and the erection of new buildings; it exists even though there are no permanent maintenance personnel such as mechanics, electricians and cooks. Everything is done by Sirius and, added to the fact that each Sirius man has around six to eight months of field duty during the year when he is either on patrol with a sledge or a motor boat, this undoubtedly makes Sirius the busiest and most active field unit in the Danish defence.

That such a small group manages to maintain this whole operation represents, I feel, quite an impressive achievement. I will therefore write a little about how the community at Daneborg functions and, perhaps, there may be something here that other communities might find instructive.

Certain conditions have to be met in order for the Daneborg cooperative to be able to cope with the task. Firstly, everyone has simply to do their best, whatever the time of day or night, without the motive of extra pay or anything more than the reward of doing the necessary jobs well.

There must not be too much emphasis on whether individuals do more or less in a given situation or at a certain time; we all have moments when, for one reason or another, we are not at our best.

Everyone must share their knowledge and insight into how best to do things. If one person makes a mistake, there is no reason why that mistake should be made again by anyone.

It is also often necessary for an individual to get on with things when needed, without waiting for the help of others.

Last but not least, none of the cooperative's members must consider themselves too good for a job, no matter what that job is or what kind of work the person normally does.

If these conditions are met, as I believe they are at Daneborg, there are really no limits to what can be achieved.

If any one of us experiences problems with a job and has to ask for help, there is always someone who is prepared to give a hand, even when busy with his own tasks.

The repetitive work that has to be done every day is organised into different rotas and for larger projects, the division of labour is necessarily pre-planned. Even though all the members of this cooperative are military personnel, formal discipline is not really necessary because self-discipline is a matter of course.

The reader may wonder why I take time to write about such things instead of getting straight on with the good stories about life at Daneborg. I have often thought, since that time, about how great the difference is between the members of the Daneborg community and similar communities in Denmark, notwithstanding the fact that patrol members have such a range of differing personalities and come from so many different backgrounds.

In short, I discovered at Sirius, not just as a member of the patrol but in every respect, an enormous sense of personal freedom and a quality of life which I have not felt anywhere else. I am convinced that this is, to a large extent, due to the freedom to take one's own decisions and the clear understanding that, at the same time, everyone takes responsibility for their actions.

There is a profound pleasure in knowing that one's own efforts are important to the smooth working and well-being of everyone in the community. One knows that the work is appreciated, even though it is not necessary for this to be spelled out every time. Sometimes it becomes clear, when starting on some problem or other, that there may be a degree of risk involved and in this case it could be vital for everyone concerned to have trust in their ability to solve the problem correctly — the first time!

Now let me tell a little more of the way in which the Sirius society functions year after year, in spite of the lack of professional technical skills among the new arrivals.

The clue to this is 'tradition' and by this is meant that as soon as a new Sirius man arrives at Daneborg, he will follow a Sirius man from the previous year, an old hand, who can help him in his daily tasks and at the same time teach him how things are done. From time to time, there is a switch around so that each new Sirius man comes to know almost all of his colleagues' jobs.

This daily work at Daneborg is split into different areas of responsibility and, to take care of these, each is taken on by two men, one an old hand and one a new recruit; a master and an apprentice, you might say. I will describe the tasks briefly to show the sorts of things people have to do while they are home at the station and not out on patrol.

The Chief — in charge of the patrol

The Chief is in overall charge and he is the exception that proves the rule because he is alone in doing this job. Probably he will be a patrol man with more than the usual two years of service behind him. Typically, he will have had two seasons as an ordinary patrol man in Northeast Greenland, followed by a couple of years in Denmark as the assistant coordinator to Guldbrandsen, then returning to Greenland to take care of the job of chief there for another two year period.

It would be difficult for outsiders to spot him, since by his own choice he will be dressed in the same clothes as everyone else and like them, he will carry no badges of rank. The only evidence that he and the rest are in fact Sirius personnel is the Sirius badge that is sewn on the left arm of their tunics.

Unlike many other chiefs, military or civilian, he will seldom be heard giving orders because everyone knows what is to be done but, of course, he has the last word if that is what is needed.

The Chief has no privileges attached to his position and does his share of the chores like everyone else.

The Dog Man — in charge of the dogs

It is said that a dog is man's best friend and in the same fashion, the Dog Man is the dogs' best friend on Sirius; he looks after their welfare when they are not out on sledge journeys.

In the 'doghouse' or kennels, he mixes their food every day, taking responsibility for the quality and quantity. It is not his job actually to feed the dogs since each patrol man will feed his own team. On the other hand, it is his job to order the year's supplies of the various different kinds of dog food for use either on the station or on sledge journeys. Besides that, he will keep records of all the dogs, decide on the breeding programme, and carry out necessary vaccinations and treatments for sickness.

The Syndicate Man — in charge of carpentry

This is the station's chief carpenter and he guards his domain, the carpenter's shop, which is called the Syndicate (plate two).

It is this man who maintains the supplies of timber, nails, screws and so on. He keeps the tools in good order and anyone using the carpenter's shop can always get expert advice from him on how to work with wood. On the other hand, they can expect some plain talk from him if they do not clean up and leave the place tidy after use. The Syndicate Man is in charge of the maintenance of the buildings and any other job where wood must be used.

The Machine Man — in charge of machinery

He is easy to recognise with his black finger nails, sores on his hands and oil stains on his clothing. He is most often to be found at the 'Knast' ('the Camshaft') which is the nickname for the machine shop. Here he will, as a rule, be found lying on his back underneath some motor vehicle or other, with spare parts and tools spread all around. Besides the vehicles, the Machine Man is also responsible for the electricity generators, driven by diesel engines, which keep a constant supply of power to the station. He is the patrol's mechanic and blacksmith and has responsibility for water, heating and sanitation, as well as maintaining supplies of metals, tools and fuels.

The Sparky — in charge of electrical supply

This is the person who takes the power provided by the Machine Man and sees that it is distributed to those who need it. He is the person that people shout at when they get a shock from the washing machine or when any electrical equipment doesn't function properly. He has his workshop and supplies in the 'Krumtappen' (the 'Crankshaft') but can usually be seen at various points around the station with his test meter and circuit breakers. Besides being the electrician, he also has responsibility for the patrol's radio equipment and must ensure that, at any time, communication with the outside world is possible.

The Osmosis Man — in charge of water supply

This is the man who ensures that there is always a plentiful supply of fresh water in the water tanks, summer and winter; a job that has only come about in recent times now that the station is equipped with what older generation Sirius men would undoubtedly have called a 'modern gimmick', namely an osmosis plant. Briefly, this will treat salt water pumped from Young Sund and produce fresh water from it. Smart! It replaces, when it works properly of course, the old but well-known method of melting snow blocks.

The Provisions Man — in charge of food and drink

Some claim that this is the most important person on the station and not without reason, for it is his job to see that the cook always has plenty of luscious juicy steak at his disposal, and that he has what is necessary to be able to serve medium or rare with a mass of bearnaise sauce and other trimmings to the always-hungry Sirius men.

The Provisions Man can often be found in his store, surrounded by shelves filled with anything from French potatoes to Worcestershire sauce. Because of difficulties in supply, it is unfortunately rare for him to have exotics such as chinese cabbage, but tinned food he always has in large quantities.

He is the station's supermarket manager and will ensure that the food supplies will last throughout the year; he also, as part of his field of responsibility, ensures that food depots are adequately stocked and maintained out in the patrol areas.

The Slop Chest man — in charge of clothing

This man is in charge of the 'slop chest' where one can find any article of arctic clothing from among a mass of parkas, socks and underwear. Unfortunately, he usually guards his stock like a hawk and not until you show him a garment with a hole that simply cannot be repaired or a pair of completely worn-out boots, will his heart melt. Only when a sledge team is about to depart on patrol will his generosity increase, and then each person can choose exactly what clothing he finds he needs to cope with the cold conditions expected.

The Boat Man — in charge of marine transportation

The Boat Man has responsibility for the patrol's fleet and decides who will use it. He is responsible for the Sirius boats and cutters, that they are painted, fully equipped and ready for the day when the winter ice in Young Sund clears out to sea, leaving open water for the summer.

From the beginning of July, he will be working full time with scraper and paintbrush down by the fjord. Then again, he will be busy cleaning the cutters in September when all boats are taken out of the water and covered up for the winter.

The 'Nordre' Man — in charge of miscellaneous stores and chandlery

The station's ironmonger has his warehouse in 'Nordre' — a special hut where he keeps all kinds of rope, pots and pans, knives and forks, skis and much besides. In addition to keeping the station well supplied with these items and many, many other things he, like the Provisions Man, has also to ensure that the depots are well stocked with all the items that may be needed by sledge teams.

The Fire Master — in charge of all firefighting

Fire is one of the greatest fears among those who live in the Arctic, where the living accommodation is usually built of wood and where water is scarce and very difficult to work with at low temperatures.

If such an accident should happen at Daneborg, then the Fire Master is responsible for the fire pumps, hoses and breathing apparatus and must ensure that they are always ready for instant use. His task is to work out plans to deal with any outbreak of fire and to have unannounced fire drills so that each man knows what to do if the worst should happen.

That covers most of the regular jobs at Daneborg. Because they are not all equally demanding and some are only seasonal, one individual may combine two or three tasks as his regular responsibility. It also goes without saying that, even though the major station work is shared in this way, there is always masses of other work to be done. The guiding principle is to give a hand where it is needed, once one's own task is finished.

The allocation of jobs is usually according to everyone's occupation in civilian life, a carpenter becoming the Syndicate Man, a car mechanic or blacksmith the Machine Man and so on. Of course, individual wishes are taken into consideration so that if a clerk wants to become Dog Man or a farmer wants to be in charge of socks and jackets and so on, that is how it works out. It is unusual for there to be more than one or two people with specialist skills and many Sirius men come directly from college, but their lack of knowledge is soon overcome by the apprentice system, as I have already described.

I still need to mention a couple more important duties undertaken by everyone in turn, and this I can best do by taking up the tale where I left off; at the moment when we were newly arrived at Daneborg on that fine day in July.

Cooking Duty

After a quick look around our new surroundings, we are told that the cook has lunch ready. We gather in 'Sirihus' ('hus' being the Danish word for house), the building that houses the patrol's kitchen and dining room, or mess.

Within the mess room there is a large lunch table laid out with a variety of dishes that is surprisingly wide, considering that most are made from tinned or frozen foods. It is clear from this that the lack of fresh food does not result in a boring diet. The cook has not quite finished setting the warm food on the table and, through the small serving hatch, we can see him putting the final touches to it.

One of us newcomers pulls out a chair from the table and is about to sit down when an old hand, standing nearby, taps him on the shoulder and says: "Hold on; you are about to get yourself the cook's job, though of course you know nothing about that yet".

"How is that?" asks the newcomer, as he hurriedly pushes the chair back in its place.

"Well, you see", continues the old hand, "here on Sirius, we have some rules and traditions. I had better tell you about a few of them while we wait for the food. The cook's job, which most of us would rather not have to do, is taken in turn by each of us for a week at a time".

He doesn't say that this includes the chief also, but it is understood.

"There are certain rules for the cook's job which you will need to remember", he continues. "The first is that one does not sit down at the table until the cook has invited you to do so, and the second is that the cook has the place right here at the end of the table where you were about to sit down," he nodded to the man, "and only the cook sits there. For a third thing, you must not '*mifle*' before ten o'clock in the evening."

"*Mifle*?", asks the newcomer.

"Ah, yes. To '*mifle*' is to go into the kitchen on your own and help yourself to an evening snack. This is allowed, but only after 10 pm and we call it mifling. Then there is just one more thing, which is perhaps the most important of all."

"What is that?" we ask anxiously.

"There are never any complaints about the cook's food on Sirius."

"And, what happens if someone does complain , or if we break some of the other taboos you have mentioned?" I ask.

"Then the cook's job is yours with instant effect," chuckles the old hand.

At that moment the cook comes into the mess, puts the last dishes on the table and says, "Please eat, gentlemen".

We all say a polite thank you and as newcomers, sit carefully at the table, wondering if there is still some custom or other that we have not yet been told about and looking surreptitiously at the others to see what they do.

There is plenty of talk around the table, because Gulli (the old hands use this nickname without hesitation for Guldbrandsen who has, meanwhile, changed from his commander's uniform into a set of bleached blue fatigues) is interested to hear what the old hands have to say about their sledge journeys; something that they need very little encouragement to talk about in these surroundings.

Much is said about the dangerous situations that people have found themselves in; about the blizzards, what the travelling conditions have been like and, of course, about the sledge dogs, sledge dogs, and more sledge dogs. Meanwhile we, the newcomers, sit silently, listening carefully to the talk which is exciting enough even though the meaning is sometimes difficult to follow because of so many technical and slang words.

After roughly an hour, the chief breaks off the conversation by hinting that it is about time to get back to some work.

"By the way, it is Friday tomorrow," he says, "and on Friday evening the cook changes places so one of you new people may as well take over in the kitchen ... hm ... let me see ..." he looks around the table. "Well, is that not something for you, Mikkel?"

I will freely admit that it is not quite what I have in mind. I rather fancy myself exercising my talents outside in the fine summer weather, perhaps patrolling around the mountains or something like that. The kitchen is not exactly the debut I envisaged as a new Sirius man; but of course I nod and say to the Chief that I am ready.

At this point I should confess that my total experience in cookery amounts to boiling eggs or making porridge, and the prospect of cooking for ten to 20 people for an entire week is daunting. I think to myself that, if the chief knew a little more about my skills in that department, he might suggest someone else.

"On Saturday, you will have one of the old hands helping you in the kitchen, Mikkel, because in the summer we normally have a large dinner every other Saturday; if we have time for it", he adds.

Aha, I think; the traditional Danish *smorgasbord*; what luck. There should be no problem to set a few herrings on the table, slice up some ham and make a couple of warm dishes. I am still blissfully unaware of what a Sirius man expects for his Saturday dinner.

At 10 o'clock on Friday evening I am ready to take over the duties of cook. A heavy smell of cleanser greets me as I put my head around the kitchen door and I can see the out-going cook, sweating hard, armed with a cloth in each hand with which he is attacking a large gas stove.

"It will be another half hour before I'm finished," he says, breathing hard.

At the same time the old hand, who is to help me the following day, passes by and asks me if I have thought about what I am going to serve at dinner on the Saturday evening. "Well, yes I have," I say, thinking myself well prepared, and show him a list on which I have written out: salt herring, fried fish, pork steaks with soft onions, sliced ham, cheese and fruit.

"That looks OK for a start, but I think we shall have to add a couple of warm dishes and some salads to it," he says, after some thought.

"Er... warm dishes... I thought the fried fish and the pork ...?" I stammer, pointing at my list.

"Yes, of course, but that is not really enough," he says, "because up here we have to live every day for six to eight months in the year on porridge, tuna fish in tomato sauce, and pemmican. When, at last, we have the opportunity, we like to have something a little less ordinary. Food comes to mean a lot to most of us when the meals we eat are often the only real pleasure in a long day's routine. Let's sit down in the mess for a moment and add a few things so that we can ask the Provisions Man to supply the ingredients."

A few things! I think he writes without a break, for ten minutes until my piece of paper is completely filled on both sides. Finally, he gives it back to me and I stare in disbelief at what he is written there: Chickens, steaks, and many other things that one could see on a Danish dinner table. Then follow the salads; crab salad, mackerel salad, prawn salad, fruit salad and many more (some with long names), cheese and ham and various accessories. What he means by 'various accessories' I do not dare to try to guess, but I imagine it might be rather a lot!

"Are you sure you have thought of everything?" I ask him, with a touch of irony.

He doesn't notice the hint and says: "No, now that you mention it, I see I have forgotten roast beef." He manages to find a place to write it down on the piece of paper.

"Now all you need do is give the note to the Provisions Man, Mikkel, and he will see to it that all the ingredients are brought over here; I will meet you in the kitchen tomorrow at half past five."

"That's early," I comment, since breakfast is not to be served until 8 o'clock.

"It is necessary because we shall bake some bread and Danish pastries."

Slightly shocked, I find the Provisions Man who reads the note carefully. "I'll fix that," he says very helpfully, "but would you not like to have some sausages too?"

Sausages?!

"Good grief, we have completely forgotten those," I say seriously, and head back to the kitchen.

The cook has just finished washing the floor, everything is gleaming and there isn't a greasy spot to be seen anywhere. On the other hand, he looks almost exhausted. We stand and talk a little and then, when the floor has dried, he says: "Well, it is ready for you."

"OK", I say.

"Are you not going to check if everything is clean enough?"

"I simply wouldn't know where to start," I answer with complete honesty.

"Fine, then the kitchen is yours, Mikkel," and, with a look of relief on his face as though I have just saved him another couple of hours of cleaning, he is gone before I have a chance to change my mind.

Well, if he has cheated he has been very clever because, once I am left alone in my kitchen, I cannot in all honesty find any place that has not been thoroughly cleaned.

I think a bit about what I am going to prepare for breakfast next day but agree with myself that it is better left until the morning when the old hand can tell me where everything is. Instead, I just stand there a while and reflect on the odd ways in which chance affects one's life.

Why did it have to be me that was chosen to be the first of us newcomers to start in the kitchen? It is, to say the least, unlucky because dealing with food was never one of my strong points. I feel sympathy for the rest of the mess, still blissfully ignorant of the tortures they are about to have to face. They will, without doubt, come to hate me for the rest of their days since, as is well known, it is first impressions that count. I can almost imagine the headlines in the newspapers back home in Denmark saying something like 'Sirius man sent home because of incompetence as a cook', or 'Three Sirius men die of food poisoning and four others in a critical condition'. Further down in the article there will be something along the lines of ... 'and it came to a fight when the cook, for the fifth day in a row, served oatmeal porridge. Well-informed sources state that ...'

Maybe it won't turn out that badly. I take some comfort from what one of the old hands said to me earlier in the day: "Up here you can do three times as much as you think you can and ten times as much as your mother thinks you can". I had also, in the days leading up to departure from Denmark, written down some of my mother's recipes in a notebook and besides, there is a large shelf full of cookery books in the kitchen. That is encouraging.

I look at my watch; half past eleven. I had better go to bed. On the way out through the door I bump into two other newcomers like myself.

"Come and join us for a walk?" they are cruel enough to ask.

What a temptation on this calm sunny evening. We stand for a moment outside the Sirihus and enjoy the marvellous view out over the fjord then, as they walk off, I hear one of them say with a sigh of contentment: "Isn't it great that we shall be in such a fantastic place from now on?"

"Hmm," I mutter and can think only about my coming week in the kitchen.

The alarm clock is ringing. I wake with a groan and remember that I am expected to have breakfast ready with fresh-baked bread and pastries in about two and a half hours.

Out of bed, a quick wash, clothes on and then over to Sirihus. As I approach, I hear music from inside; the old hand has already arrived, put a record on the player and is humming to himself as he makes the bread. I stand and watch him for a moment, not knowing just where to start my career as a cook.

"What shall we serve for breakfast?" I ask.

"That is completely up to you" is the helpful answer. "You are the cook and the cook is master in his kitchen; I would suggest fried bacon and eggs, boiled eggs, bread and beer soup and oatmeal porridge. We are used to having a few different things, not too much of each but in such a way that everyone has a choice. One thing is certain; we will have eggs because they are the first we have seen here for five months."

I set about finding all the different ingredients. Eggs and bacon, pots and pans. The old hand tells me where to find various things when I cannot find them myself, and he also shows me the best way of preparing the bread and pastries.

"Where is the milk?"

"Out in the pantry," he answers.

"Isn't that too warm?" I was going to ask; then, of course, I realise that it is not milk in cartons that I am going to be finding, as at home, but dried powder that has to be mixed. I find the powder and start to mix it, my helper saying that it tastes better with a little vanilla-sugar blended in. In no time at all, the clock says 7.30 and I need to set the table.

How long until the bread is ready? What about the eggs?

A little later the old hand says it is 7.50 and I should wake people with a call over the intercom. The last ten minutes are taken up with setting out the food, then people began to arrive and, by 7.59, everything is in place. Phew!

I take off my apron, go into the mess and stand for a moment, wondering why people don't sit down and start eating. They look at me expectantly. Of course, I am cook.

"Eh ... oh, of course, please go ahead; help yourselves."

During breakfast, I chat with the old hand to find out what are the normal meal times. I learn that I have to serve no fewer than six meals between 8 o'clock in the morning and 9 o'clock in the evening. That brings it home to me that I will not have much of a problem with waiting for the time to pass during my first week with Sirius.

Right now, it is the evening's dinner that is concerning me most. I cannot see how I am going to prepare that and, at the same time, prepare all these other meals.

"Relax," says the old hand: "After we have enjoyed a peaceful and leisurely breakfast, we will start preparing things that can be got ready in advance, cut the meat, prepare the chickens and so on, and get everything ready for the oven."

It sounds easy enough when he puts it that way; the problem is that I have never tried to prepare a chicken in my life. We start, and soon I run into other surprises. I will have to mix up various different salads; I have seen all the ingredients except for one thing — the mayonnaise.

"We ran out some time back, so we mix it ourselves," comes back the answer to my question. That is certainly something I haven't foreseen and I will first have to find out how to mix it before I can go on to the unknown world of actually preparing salads. I consult the book again, wondering if I first have to prepare the ingredients for the mayonnaise, but luckily the answer seems to be 'no'.

"How many grams do you think I should mix?" I ask.

"Um... about four to six kilos," comes the answer.

Four to six kilos of mayonnaise for dinner! I suppose it has to be true if he says so. It fits quite nicely with the recipe; just multiply everything by ten. The final result looks pretty good when it is mixed and seasoned. God knows how many calories there are in such a concoction!

Now for the salads. Open cans of prawns, crabs and mussels. Mix the dressings; oops, it is almost time for coffee break. Put on a large kettle of water for the coffee, tea and cocoa. Put the cups on the table.

"Do they have anything to eat at coffee time?" I ask, and am prepared for the worst.

"No, they can just have some of fru Kjeldsen's cookies" says my helper, to my surprise and relief.

We take our own coffee in the kitchen while we work on at full speed. My shirt is soaked in sweat and, to show that I am a beginner, I am already covered with spatters of mayonnaise and other things. I think of the old saying, 'The best cook makes the least washing up', and look at the mountain of dirty dishes and utensils that I have already managed to produce.

By 11 o'clock, it is time to start preparing lunch which has to be served at 1 pm.

All the other things we are working on have to be covered over with plastic foil and we get out the sliced meats and jams, mix the fruit juice and so on. I start to hate this kitchen and wonder if the madness will ever end. How is the old hand, my helper, able to stay so calm and look so relaxed. He even has time to change the record now and again, or rather start it again, for at that point we have heard Abba's *Arrival* the entire morning, first one side and then the other. He has just received it with his mail. The record is almost a year old at home, but out here in the wilderness it is brand new. Here we go again: 'You are the dancing queen,' at about 117 decibels. Myself, I feel more like a wet cloth!

With a pan of improvised hash in my hand, I just manage to reach the mess by 1 o'clock and say: "Please, go ahead". I sit at the table but have no appetite to eat anything myself.

"Hey, don't you like the food you have cooked?" asks the man beside me.

The evening's dinner is due at eight o'clock and by half past six I can almost begin to believe that we may be ready. The joint of pork has been in the oven for a couple of hours, four kilos of fruit salad are standing in bowls with chocolate and accessories, and all the other things are ready to go in the oven. We take a short break to clean up and have a quick shower. I really need it.

Back to the kitchen. Turning everything on, we fry steaks and burgers while our hands move like sticks in the hands of a drummer. Turn up the heat here, turn it down there. As things become ready, they are put into the warm ovens to wait, although it feels as though it is about 90 degrees celsius in the kitchen itself.

By a quarter to eight, as if by some miracle, we have cooked and fried and got everything ready and the table is laid with white tablecloths to show that it is a special day. People begin to arrive and there is laughter and good humour in the mess. We have mixed a bowl of punch and, while everyone has a drink of that, we bring in the food. It fills the table.

"Well, we have another tradition in Sirius," says someone, as we sit at the table, "which is that the first toast is always to the cooks".

They raise their glasses and call '*Skål*' (cheers), for the cooks.

It is well past midnight when I walk over to my room, still with the sounds of 'Dancing Queen' in the background. I feel good, but so tired that I think I am asleep before my head hits the pillow.

Next morning it is back to the kitchen but, surprisingly, the kitchen and the mess look nice and clean; the people from last year who have left Sirihus during the night have, following another tradition, cleaned and tidied everything. All the uneaten food has been wrapped up and put in the fridge so that it can be used in the next few days. Nothing is wasted. Any unwanted food is put into a special bucket for the dogs, which the dog man collects every day and uses to feed to the puppies and nursing bitches.

Because Sirius men are in the field for so long every year, living under primitive conditions, they set a high value on a clean and tidy station and there is always a 'handyman' whose job is rather like that of the cook in that it is shared around between everyone, but is done by two men for one day at a time.

Straight after breakfast, the handyman team starts the cleaning, washing, and vacuuming in Sirihus, before moving on to the shared facilities like toilets, laundry and so on; not that there is a lot to do because things mostly stay very clean, but it is a daily routine. Depending on the time of year, there may be snow to clear from the outside doors, or sweeping outside. Once these chores are done, the handymen for the day can get on with their own tasks, with only the washing-up to do later on after the three main meals. Peeling potatoes is another chore for them, if potatoes are on the menu; the rest, of course, is the cook's job.

My week on cooking duty was most definitely a busy time. I never had a moment to get bored during that first week; cooking for ten to twenty people who expected six meals or snacks a day never left me time to get bored and, even though it became more or less routine after a while, I seldom found I had the energy to do anything more than go straight to bed after the day's work was done.

I have related this story of the Saturday dinner seen from the cook's point of view, although perhaps it paints a slightly unbalanced picture. On a normal day we lived like normal people except, perhaps, that we ate a bit more than the average man at home and we always had a choice of two dishes for each meal. There was clearly a big variation between different Sirius men in their abilities and liking for the cook's job. Some liked it a lot and had a real talent for it, producing excellent and satisfying food with the very limited resources on hand.

Amongst my own year's intake, one man was a real wizard and it was easy to put on a couple of kilos in weight while he was cook, thanks to the variety of breads at every meal-time and the large assortment of fresh-baked pastries. For one Saturday dinner at midsummer, he served no fewer than 16 different warm dishes and, on that occasion, we had just returned from four and a half months of continuous sledge patrol. Even so, it took us around nine hours to eat our way through the entire meal! The other side of the coin was that there were, of course, some who took advantage of the fact that we never complained about the food.

Even though the cook could select whatever menu he wished for the day, he still had to follow a few rules such as providing at least two different dishes for the main midday meal. It was also a rule that there had to be white bread for lunch, but there was nothing to say that the bread had to be good quality. It was held by some that the better the bread, the more of it people ate and therefore the more that had to be baked! These folk produced bread that could have been used as a hammer in the blacksmith's workshop and, in this way, only had to bake once during their cook week!

In the whole of my time with Sirius, I can remember only one occasion when someone criticised the cook directly and, even though the criticism was not without good cause, he had to take responsibility for it. To wild cheering, the cook jumped up and demanded a court martial at once; the verdict was 'guilty' and the critic was sent forthwith to the kitchen!

Another tradition was that everyone was obliged to taste all the delicacies that the cook served; not a large portion of course, but at least a small taste which one was honour-bound to finish.

Personally, I think it was a good system but it could lead to some odd situations. In the evening for instance, it was normal for the cook to serve some home-baked cakes with the coffee. Most of us had got recipes sent from home for just such an eventuality and it became quite an experience in eating traditional baking from different regions of Denmark. For the most part, the results were really excellent.

One of my colleagues was renowned for his first-class baking and one evening, when he was the duty cook, we arrived at the mess as usual at around nine pm. There was a beautiful-looking cake standing ready on the table. The cook, who was still in the kitchen, called for us to go ahead, so we quickly cut ourselves large slices, sat down at the table and started to eat ... ??!!

After the first mouthful, it was clear that all was not right. It was a ginger cake, there was no doubt about that but it seemed as though the cook might have mis-read kilos for grams!

Sitting at the table, we looked at one another and all came to realise that this cake was definitely something special. We were calculating rapidly whether or not we could get to the waste bucket and back to the table again to resume our normal places, before the cook arrived on the scene. We could hear him coming in from the kitchen. There was no time. He appeared and we greeted him as normal, just as though everything was fine, all the while watching him covertly as he cut himself a large slice. He sat down with a rather distant look on his face, probably preoccupied with thinking out the next day's menu, and we all waited with baited breath. He gasped and jumped in his seat as he took his first mouthful, and we had to look the other way to avoid catching each other's eyes and laughing. However, the cook carried on eating rapidly and we could see from the corners of our eyes that he turned his head slowly to watch us. More people arrived in the mess and he watched each new arrival carefully, but they were all used to keeping their feelings under strict control, at least while the cook was present. Somehow everyone managed to keep a straight face, although the tension was nearly unbearable.

With the help of large volumes of coffee, we all managed to eat our large slices and, when the last man was finished, we were able to look at each other again. Smiles began to appear and soon everyone was roaring with laughter. For several minutes, no-one could do anything but laugh helplessly.

The strange part of that whole event was that no-one ever put into words the reason why we were laughing so much!

Sirius life was full of traditions, as I have related, and one of these concerned the cook's duties on Friday night. At this point he was expected to serve a special cream layer-cake for his last evening's coffee time. Usually, this was left to the very last minute with the result that it was often not a very good effort, or else it was one of those pre-packed confections, hurriedly opened, and containing gigantic amounts of synthetic cream and jelly. Needless to say, it was still eaten!

Everything comes to an end, even a stint as cook with Sirius and it may be late Friday evening or more likely Friday night before the cook can finish his big clean-up. No matter what the time, the moment the cook can look forward to is when he can say to the next man on the rota: "OK, now it is your turn!"

Summer in Greenland

Summer in Northeast Greenland is brief but intense. The sun begins to have some power by April, increasing steadily until, by May and June, the days can be quite warm. Snow that is not permanent does not disappear until the beginning of July and it is at this point that winter really loses its grip and summer rapidly takes over. It has been said that in Northeast Greenland, summer arrives in a single night and that once the arctic summer has started, it exerts its astonishing power over natural events for the full twenty four hours. Day by day, the ground changes from a covering mat of dead plant remains to a field of new flowers. A newcomer to the country, or a short-term visitor with recent memories of gardens and fields in Denmark, would probably not be that impressed by the small size of these plants and flowers; they are very much smaller than examples we are used to seeing in more southerly climates and many lie flat on the ground, or reach up to no more than the height of one's ankle. But for those who have lived through the long arctic winter and day after day, experienced the iron-hard grip of nature for eight long months, it is difficult to believe that any living thing can survive in such a place. Suddenly, the flowers are there as living proof that survival is possible.

In the short time that the plants are growing, Sirius men are also busy. The flora coming to life is a sign that the permafrost is retreating a little below the ground surface and that there is a short opportunity to dig foundations or put up new buildings. On the whole, the short arctic summer is the only time when it is possible to repair and improve man's defences in the battle to survive the rigours of winter. Once frost starts again, and that can happen even before the end of August, the cold begins to regain control and once more, men are forced back into a survival mentality to take their chances as best they can.

Even though the patrol functions the whole year round without permanent service personnel, temporary help is available during the busy summertime in the shape of visiting specialists; there are tasks which, believe it or not, Sirius men have difficulty in doing themselves! The first priority for this help is often radio communications, even though there are sometimes years when a radio mechanic such as myself is serving with the patrol. The testing and adjustment of the radio equipment for optimum performance is highly specialised work, something I can vouch for personally having had that responsibility. Certainly, there were some problems with the radios that I could fix using my own knowledge and experience, but I did not have the training or, for that matter, the time to install and set up new equipment. In order to keep everything up to scratch, it was customary for two technicians, Hans Jensen and Stig Andersen from the navy, to come to Daneborg at the same time as the new station personnel. They were nicknamed the summer sledge team or, for a while, Hansel and Gretel.

There are, in fact, a lot of problems connected with the construction and use of radio equipment in the Arctic. At temperatures below minus 40°C, most materials lose their elasticity and become brittle like glass, a factor that causes problems with the fabrication simply because it may not have been taken into account when the equipment was designed. This problem is not confined to radio equipment and affects much that is used in the Arctic. Typically, it may only be one or two small details that need altering to make the difference between an article being completely useless and the same item working almost perfectly under arctic conditions.

In the case of the radio gear, the performance of the equipment was steadily improved by the 'summer sledgers', largely through learning from the experiences of the Sirius men in winter.

Imaqa (maybe) is a commonly used eskimo saying when referring to anything that lies in the future. They know what they are talking about and living in Northeast Greenland, it is unwise to plan more than one day ahead if disappointment is to be avoided; the weather is just too unpredictable at all times of the year. It comes to be accepted that what cannot be done one year may be possible the next. This is not an excuse for laziness but simple acceptance of the facts of living under arctic conditions.

Even though the Sirius men work, as a rule in summertime, from 8 am to 8 pm (apart from a Sunday off from time to time) it would be impossible for them to get everything done without outside help. A good example of this was the erection of a new building for the station, as happened in 1978 when a new carpenter's shop had to be built to replace the old one that burnt down the previous autumn. This was to be started and finished in one summer; it could not be left half completed once work had to stop for the winter. Since the carpenter's shop was a very important part of the station, two extra carpenters and an electrician were sent north to help. This in itself was nothing unusual, but the events leading up it are worth relating.

October 1977 was quite an ordinary October, with frost throughout the twenty four hours and the dark nights well-established. There was already quite a lot of snow and the landscape was completely white. All the patrol members were gathered at Daneborg since the fjord had begun to freeze and use of the boats was no longer possible; on the other hand the sea ice was not yet thick enough to sledge on.

The Sirius coordinator, the home-bound patrol members and all the summer's technical support personnel had left the previous month and we overwintering men were on our own. As usual, life on the station had become a little more relaxed for, although it is enjoyable to have guests, helping ones at that, it is nice to get back to the normal routine again after they leave.

It was still very busy on the station, with much to complete before the winter and many preparatory jobs to complete before the start of the actual sledge patrols. It had been particularly busy in the carpenter's shop where people had been working 18 hours a day on building new dog sledges, each team of two men building a new sledge in approximately one week. It was an important job, the new sledges being needed to replace those worn out after two years of hard use. All the new members had to gain experience in the actual building of the sledges so that, if something broke (as it invariably did) when out on a sledge journey, they would know how to fix it.

The first of the new sledges was already completed and the next almost ready in the carpenter's shop, on the fateful night of 7 October.

The evening had been relatively dark even for that time of year. Heavy, bad weather clouds were visible to the north and during the night a north wind had risen; the normal wind direction for bad weather at Daneborg. We had gone to bed at about midnight, as usual, apart from two men who were still working in the carpenter's shop to fix the last details on their new sledge. By two o'clock in the morning they were finished at last, after a week of concentrated work. Their sledge was ready for naming the next day, so they turned out the lights and went to bed.

At about five o'clock that morning I was woken abruptly by someone shouting: "The carpenter's shop is on fire!" I was quickly out of my bed and awake and would have turned on the light, but there was no electric power. A lot of noise was coming from the other rooms in the building, where people were stumbling around trying to find their clothes in the darkness. Things were not made any easier by the confusion of sleepy people trying to hurry, getting the wrong leg into their trousers and so on. Everyone stumbled out of their rooms to try to find out what on earth was going on, hoping that it was just a bad practical joke. Of course, no-one would make such a joke and as we rounded the corner of the hut, we could see that the carpenter's shop was already a mass of flames. Perhaps our military training helped, but whether this is true or not, it was less than three minutes before everyone was at the scene.

In spite of the seriousness of the situation, there was no panic. The fire chief took command and each of us began to do our job, rolling out the hoses, getting the fire pumps started and connected to the big water tanks. Two Sirius men with breathing apparatus were already kitted up.

It was soon clear that the carpenter's shop was lost because of the strong wind. The fire must have started on the lee side and that gave us hope that we might at least save some of the contents of the building, but flames were spreading very fast through the dry timbers of which the building was made. The two men with breathing apparatus managed to save our supply of eggs and some of the fruit, vegetables and potatoes which were in a frost-free provisions store inside the building. In the end, however, they were beaten back by the flames. After that, all that could be done was to try to prevent the fire from spreading to other buildings nearby. Fortunately the nearest, the 'Upper' house, was ten metres away and in little danger, thanks to the wind direction.

There were, however, problems on the other side of the building where two large fuel tanks were sited to supply the heating plant in the carpenter's shop. Because of heat from the burning building, leaks were developing in the pipework as pressure built up, causing fountains of oil to spurt out. Something had to be done; even though there was only a small chance of the cold oil igniting, we didn't want to take any chances. All valves were shut off and snow was shovelled onto the overheated pipes, while asbestos cloth was used to shield the tanks themselves. It was very warm work but the result was a fall in the oil pressure in the pipes and then we could relax a little.

As the first grey light of dawn arrived, the wind began to die away and the bad weather moved on south of Daneborg. The fire was now under control and, since I was the electrician, I went with the mechanic to see if the power generators could be started again. As it turned out, this was quite a difficult task but it was vital to get something done as quickly as possible before all sorts of other problems began to develop in the other buildings. Water pipes would soon begin to freeze and do even more damage. After some tinkering here and there, we succeeded.

Two hours after the outbreak of the fire, the flames were dying out and our carpenter's shop was just a ruin; a pile of smoking ashes. While two men stayed behind to guard against any renewed outbreak, the rest of us were able to retire to the mess for breakfast and a discussion on the situation. We were a colourful bunch. Everyone had red faces from the heat and the cold. Some had had their eyebrows burnt off and it was funny now to see people with their clothes inside out and in disarray, boots on the wrong feet and so on. Now that we could relax a little, we were able to laugh at the comical sight. Not surprisingly, those who found it hardest to recover their good humour were the two who had spent the whole of the preceding week building their new sledge, now no more than ashes and hot, bent metal. I myself had lost a brand new eight metre dog whip which had taken a lot of my free time to make, but this was a relatively minor loss and we all felt a lot of sympathy for the two sledge builders.

Several things had to be done straight away. In the first place, the Sirius coordinator and other authorities in Denmark had to be notified. The fire meant that they would have to start immediately to plan for a replacement building the following summer. Funds would have to be raised, engineering plans drawn up and materials ordered; a big job, all to be done before the next supply ship left Denmark in about eight month's time.

For us, the fire would certainly mean some problems and discomfort until the ship returned. We had lost almost all of our woodworking tools and materials and would therefore have to plan to repair old sledges as best we could, instead of building new ones.

In spite of our salvage efforts, we had lost quite a lot of our fresh provisions and would have to put up with shortages of milk, fresh fruit and vegetables. There would be no drink at Christmas time since the whole of our beer, wine and spirit supplies had gone up in the flames. Unlucky to say the least but, looking on the bright side, we would soon be out on patrol and would only have to be at Daneborg for about two of the eight months until next summer.

Re-building of our new carpenter's shop in the summer of 1978 saw the realisation of all this planning and preparation, but a lot of hard work was needed to overcome the problems that are always encountered during the erection of new buildings in the high Arctic. Chief of these is permafrost, the permanently frozen state of the ground in Arctic regions, down to a depth of many metres. Before any foundations can be dug out, the surface layers must first be thawed. Even then, the hut cannot be built to sit directly on top of the permanently frozen ground; heat from the house would soon start to thaw the ground underneath and the foundations would then become unstable. For these reasons, the house must either be supported on pillars to allow cold air to circulate underneath, or it must be built with a thick layer of extremely good insulation between it and the ground.

The replacement for our burnt building was supplied as prefabricated sections, already fully insulated. The whole process of putting it up, including installation of the services such as water, heating and electricity, took only five weeks, and by the time the summer workers went home, we had a brand new Syndicate. All that remained to be done was to move in the new tools and equipment which had also arrived on the supply ship; soon done by the Syndicate Man and his helpers.

The ship's visit

The arrival of the yearly supply ship has always been one of the high points of life in Northeast Greenland. This was especially true in earlier times before the days of radio, when the ship was usually the only contact with the outside 'civilised' world for an entire year.

Towards the end of July, when the fjord ice starts to break up and drift out to the open sea, over-wintering folk such as trappers and hunters began, in the old days, to watch the outer coast for any sign of the ship arriving. It would bring provisions for the coming year, news from the outer world, and perhaps new people to stay for the ensuing winter. It could also be that one or two would be waiting for the ship to take them home, having found the prospect of another long winter and its loneliness more than they could bear to contemplate.

The days of the hunters and trappers are long gone, the last real hunter having left Northeast Greenland in the fifties, but now, just as in the old days, it is impossible to predict from the date the ship leaves Denmark exactly when it will arrive in East Greenland. The reason for this is that the pack ice which guards the East Greenland coast is just as difficult and unpredictable for a modern ship as it was for the old seal-hunters with only their mast-head lookouts to aid navigation. Of course, the task of finding a way through the pack-ice is far less arduous in a modern ship, thanks to such developments as the reconnaissance helicopter and satellite photography, but in spite of these aids, there are still years when the ice conditions are difficult enough to prevent a modern ship from reaching the coast. Such a year was 1965, when the Sirius station at Daneborg could not be relieved. The weather station at Danmarkshavn, Daneborg's neighbour 300 km to the north, has experienced four such occasions when the ship could not get in until the following year.

The last days before the arrival of a ship and its progress through the pack ice is nowadays followed eagerly through radio reports. This means that the traditional welcome can be prepared well in advance, ready for the day when the ship finally arrives in the open water of Young Sund and drops anchor opposite Daneborg. Welcoming the ship does not mean just going down to the beach and waving flags and shouting. Though there may be nothing wrong with that as a greeting, people have, over the years perfected some more impressive ways of expressing their feelings of welcome. They make a 'ship's bomb'.

At a safe distance from the station, the mechanics have been collecting barrels of old oil, gasoline and so on throughout the winter. The barrels are built up into quite a pile, with some other ingredients such as old signal flares and explosives added by the person who has responsibility for the event. The moment the ship drops anchor down in the fjord, this man lights the fire and runs quickly to safety. After enough time to get well clear, which depends on how violent he expects the bomb to be, he detonates the whole lot with an ear-splitting bang, and an enormous mushroom cloud rises hundreds of metres into the sky. It looks pretty impressive and, on the ship's bridge where of course this tradition is well known, the ships siren is blown full blast. In this time-honoured way, the old ties between shore station and supply ship are renewed, men can greet each other after the year's separation and the station's relief, which this event is called, can begin. In the three summers I was with Sirius, the relief ship was always *Thala Dan*, one of the fleet of well-known red polar ships operated by Lauritzen Lines.

There is no jetty at Daneborg, so the ship has to anchor about 100 metres offshore (plate seven). All the supplies and provisions, amounting to some 100-150 tonnes, are then ferried to the beach in two cargo launches which shuttle to and fro, while fuel for the next year is pumped ashore through a long pipeline.

All this takes three or four hectic days since no ice skipper wants to keep his ship inside the great pack-ice belt longer than is absolutely necessary; it can be so difficult to escape again. At Daneborg, everything that is not absolutely vital is stopped and all the Sirius men, including Gulli, work hard from early morning until late in the evening; even the technicians and summer helpers are recruited to help work cargo. The only person to escape is the cook who is fully occupied running around in his kitchen, trying to prepare enough food to keep a lot of hard-working and hungry people from starving.

Throughout these days the two launches, each manned by two crew, ply back and forth between ship and shore, the ship slowly rising higher out of the water and Daneborg itself changing. Boxes and containers lie everywhere and, even though the unpacking is fairly organised, the station gradually comes to look something like a cross between the destruction of Jerusalem and a Persian goat market. To add to the impression of bedlam, there is much shouting and advice amongst the folk handling the fuel pipeline because of the danger presented by ice drifting to and fro in the fjord. Many times, the pumping of fuel must be halted in case a piece of drifting ice threatens to tear the floating pipes, and it cannot be re-started until the threat has been averted. It is vitally important to avoid any damage to the fuel pipes not only because a spillage would cause expensive loss and interrupt the fuelling process, but also because any leaking of fuel would create serious pollution; especially critical in the cold arctic marine environment where oil does not disperse easily or quickly.

On shore, the shouts of people who have to move the containers off the trucks can also be heard from time to time, especially when it comes to lifting crates with a weight of well over 300 kg. Something like: "Who is the jerk who packed this damn box? it is as heavy as lead," will be heard all too often. Everyone knows who the curses are aimed at because, of course, it is the newcomers who packed the goods back home at Holmen. Naturally enough, they had wanted to fill all the boxes to the very top.

There is no point in getting worked up; it happens every year and at least with all the activity going on, there is plenty of help at hand. The important thing is to get all the stores ashore as quickly as possible and, in the summer of 1978, the situation would have become critical if the station had not had both a summer and a winter toilet.

The story behind this is that during the previous winter, as often happens among the men on the station, there was a kind of 'epidemic'. Those who had their own stereo equipment felt that there must be, at the very least, four large loudspeakers connected to it. This was a point of great importance to several Sirius men, that winter at least. So it came about that there were 15 or 20 very large and expensive loudspeakers of extremely high quality ordered from an export company in Denmark.

For a long time, people had waited impatiently through the spring for the arrival of these much discussed items. When, at last, the time came to unload them from the ship, it was decided that it was vitally important to get the boxes indoors and under cover as soon as possible. The building housing the winter toilet was chosen as the best place and this facility was soon put out of action by the huge pile of large, heavy boxes containing the priceless loudspeakers.

It was also in the summer of 1978 that I was one of the boat handlers, bringing in cargo from the ship. It was actually quite an easy number and not such heavy work as being in the party onshore with the job of lifting the heavy crates all day. We just had to motor back and forth, manoeuvring alongside the ship each time to receive a load of boxes as they were swung over the side by the ship's derricks.

The whole operation was carried out under the eagle eye of the bo'sun, who stood high up on the ship where he could see both the boat and the crane. From this position, he controlled the crane driver's actions with hand signals like a young bird with wooden wings. Sometimes the fog could make life difficult. That summer, we were lucky in not having any wind and rain, whereas the previous year there had been one day with so much stormy weather that even the short journey out to the ship was enough to start seasickness and get everyone in the boats completely soaked.

Once the unloading of cargo was finished, it was traditional for the captain to invite all the Sirius men on board ship for dinner, to meet the officers and crew and to thank everyone for a job well done. In '78, I almost missed out on this excellent tradition because of a rusty bolt and three tons of cement powder.

On that particular day, the last day of the relief, we had been working since six o'clock in the morning and the unloading had been going well. At four in the afternoon the ship told us that there were only ten tons of cement powder remaining to be moved, which was to make the concrete for the new carpenter's shop. The captain let us know that, as soon as we had finished unloading for the day, he would like to see us all on board for dinner, so there was just this cement standing between us and our relaxation. In the resulting haste, with two of us working the one launch, we almost lost three tons of prime Portland cement and thus also the new carpenter's shop, along with our reputations.

I said that it was a rusty bolt that caused the problem and should explain that it had all really started the previous year during a day of high wind and rain. That was a particularly gruesome day and the propeller of the outboard motor kept lifting out of the water because of the boat's violent movement. I had often pondered possible solutions to this problem during the intervening winter months and had come to the conclusion that the simplest way was to have some water in the bilges so that the boat sat a little lower in the sea. This idea found favour with the others and so we had decided to trim the boat in this way. Before unloading started this year, I had set about opening the sea cock to let in some water. Unfortunately, one of the bolts was rusted up and broke off. There was no time to fix it with the ship waiting and it seemed safe enough to carry on and leave a proper repair until there was some time to spare. Unhappily, or in some respects happily, spare time is a scarce commodity with Sirius and the unloading had gone very well until we came to the cement. The original idea of trimming the scow had been a good one but of course we had not, as things turned out, needed to do it at all in 1978, thanks to the fine weather.

We called out to the bosun that we would take all the remaining cargo in this, our final trip. At the ship's side we started loading and became in fact a bit overloaded because we were in such a hurry to finish the job. Also, the weight was really a little too far towards the stern of the boat and so the bow gradually began to lift rather high out of the water with the stern settling dangerously low. For a moment, I thought of telling the sailors to keep back the last part of the load but I had my reputation to think about! I had in any case omitted to tell my mate of the missing bolt and by this time, we had already slipped our mooring. He stood in the bow, blissfully unaware, and gazed towards the shore as we set off at full throttle to get in to land as quickly as possible.

This was not such a clever idea since the more I opened the throttle, the deeper the stern of the boat settled in the water. On the other hand, there was water coming in the whole time anyway and at maximum power we at least got nearer to the land a little quicker. The man in the bow was beginning to look suspicious but I encouraged him to believe that the boat was absolutely watertight and in no danger of sinking.

One hundred metres from the beach, I had to climb up onto the edge of the boat and stand there because the water was coming over the top of my rubber boots. A few moments later, things became even more exciting as, with a gurgling noise, the motor began to swamp.

Believe it or not, at exactly the moment we touched the shore, the motor died and the scow settled onto the sandy bottom. If it had happened a few seconds earlier, I think I would have been called some rather unflattering names by the rest of the men. As it turned out, hardly anyone noticed because, once the load of cement was lifted off the scow, it started to float again albeit without much freeboard! With the help of a pump, things were soon restored to normal and the whole episode became just one more story in a collection of lucky and unlucky events that were a part of life with Sirius. We all enjoyed our dinner on *Thala Dan* that evening, with dry feet.

Depots, depot-laying and summer guests

In summer there is always something going on at Daneborg. Down by the fjord, a group of Sirius men is busy preparing to depart on one boat trip as soon as the other boat returns. These journeys are a most important part of the summer's work and lay the foundation for the primary task of Sirius; sledge patrolling.

The purpose of the boat journeys is two fold; patrolling and depot-laying. The former is self-explanatory and is the summer equivalent of the sledge patrols, to maintain sovereignty over the area and keep account of environmental problems. The latter involves moving supplies out to strategic points and is a vitally important precursor to effective winter sledge journeys in such a large country, since only relatively limited loads of supplies for a maximum of 30 to 40 days, can be carried on a sledge. If good depots can be established not too far apart, the loads that must be carried on the sledges are reduced and so progress can be swifter and easier.

The depots contain everything necessary to keep sledge parties, both dogs and men, in good shape. They are placed generally in small travel huts, basically emergency shelters maintained for that purpose. Besides maintenance of existing depots and huts, the Sirius teams also, from time to time, establish new ones especially in northern Greenland where distances between depots have for a long time been very large.

It is only in the southern part of this huge northern area that it is possible to use boats for depot-laying. North of Wollaston Forland, boating becomes virtually impossible using Daneborg as a starting point, because the pack ice tends to lie in tightly against the coast. There is no inner complex of large ice-free fjords further north, as there is in the more southerly area around Ella Ø which is such an ideal area for boat travel throughout the summer.

In the more northerly areas, therefore, depot-laying is carried out with the help of a helicopter, making the skies around Daneborg a busy place in the summer. Sirius does not have its own helicopter and in 1977 this was chartered from the civil company Greenland Air Charter, GLACE, who in the summer time had a Bell 204 based at Mestersvig to support the local settlement at Scoresby Sund. The GLACE helicopter was also used to bring VIPs to visit Daneborg during the two summers that I was there.

In the summer of 1977, the Danish defence minister, the late Orla Møller, together with the chief of the defence department, General Knud Jørgensen, as well as their families, made a whole 24-hour visit to Sirius. On such an occasion, we did our best to show them how the patrol carried out its work throughout the year. At that time there simply were not the facilities to house ten or 15 guests overnight and so all the patrol members moved out of their private rooms and the guests used these for their overnight stay. Nowadays, of course, there are proper guest houses.

The next year, again, the defence minister visited with family and followers. This time it was a new person, Paul Søgaard, who had succeeded Orla Møller in the post. Unfortunately, the minister's visit on this occasion coincided with the arrival of the supply ship and this probably left him with the impression that there was no hospitality at all at Daneborg. It was only the chief and the coordinator, who could find a couple of hours to spare to show the guests around the station, before the helicopter flew them south again. This was genuinely bad luck, since the patrol, as is customary in Northeast Greenland, always tries to show its visiting guests the most generous hospitality that conditions permit. There are just some things that must always take the highest priority and it would be unthinkable to let a supply ship lie and wait to be unloaded because of visitors. This is a fact of life that anyone, even a VIP has to be clear about when visiting the arctic.

A summer Sunday at Daneborg

It is now the beginning of August and quite an ordinary Sunday morning during my second summer at Daneborg. No, that is not entirely true because this is a day off; the first free day for several weeks. The Chief and Gulli have decided that, since the various summer projects have gone very well, there is free time to be spared for a rest day.

Some prefer to have a morning lie-in and, for once, a bit of extra sleep, but I have chosen to get up at the usual time so that I can take a walk into the mountains around Daneborg. As well as this, I can do some of the other minor things that I do not normally have time for on a working day.

I start the day with a shower. In the summer there is no rationing of water consumption since all the streams are running freely and, if the tanks do get a little low, it is only necessary to pump in some extra temporarily from the fire reservoir behind the station.

I live in the 'Upper' House, also called 'Christiania' after a lawless district of Copenhagen by our companions who live in the 'Lower' House; both contain rooms for six people. Three newcomers and three old hands share each house, which is found to give a good balance of experience. I myself have by now become an old hand, being in my second year.

These wooden huts are quite good to live in although, in the winter storms, they can be a little cold on the windward side. At least, that is the complaint of the occupants of 'The New Society' in the Lower House, which is only to be expected from that lot! (The use of the names Upper and Lower here does in fact reflect the fact that one is slightly higher above sea level than the other but with a mildly satirical reference to the British Houses of Parliament!)

My room faces west and from the window, I have a view out over the fjord towards Clavering Ø. As I stand and gaze, it is hard to believe that it is eight km to the opposite shore. If one is not used to judging distances up here, a newcomer for instance, it would be normal to guess the distance to be no more than two km — as I myself did when I first arrived and an old hand asked me the classic question. He looked amused when I expressed surprise at the correct answer and, when he wished to repeat his success by asking how far I thought it was to a mountain called Zackenbergfjeld, I thought it looked like about five km so I said: "Maybe 20 km".

"Hm", he grumbled; "In fact, it is 22 km." So that was the end of that conversation!

To continue with my rest day, I stand and look down towards the fjord, I can see my dog team and decide to start my walk by going down to the dogs. On the way, I can go past Sirihus and get some breakfast for myself. On a free day, the cook is off duty until three in the afternoon when he will serve an extended 'brunch'.

There are only two of us in the mess; myself and the radio operator who is on duty for the day. He is on his way to the radio room to deal with the day's traffic.

While eating my breakfast, I look round at the pictures hanging on the mess walls. These are the winners of the latest photo competition. Anyone who has an ambition to try his hand at photography can use the well-equipped darkroom which is in fact next to my room. In the darkroom they can make enlargements of their best pictures for a competition which is held every July. Anyone who wishes to take part must produce their best black and white prints on the appointed evening, on subjects which can be anything to do with Northeast Greenland; the results are then judged to decide which are the nine best and these are then hung in the mess for the whole of the following year. Many of the pictures, which are normally enlarged to about 50 x 60 cm, are really good and surprisingly varied in spite of the fact that they are all taken locally.

After breakfast, I am ready to start my tour round the station. From Sirihus, it is a short walk down towards the fjord past the flagpole, the flag itself hanging limply in the calm morning weather. In summer time, the flag is easy to look after because until the sun starts to set again, it can be flown for twenty four hours a day.

Everything is so peaceful and idyllic, but only until I am a few metres past the pole and approaching my dog team on their span. One of the dogs has no doubt been keeping an eye on Sirihus and as soon as it sees that I am not going back into one of the huts, it starts to howl. This brings the whole team to its feet instantly, to join in the noisy welcome. The other teams look up and a few get to their feet, but as soon as they see that the visitor is not for them, they take no further interest and lie down again.

Before I get to my own team, I pass another span, knowing all the dog names even though I have nothing to do with them. It is really a matter of honour to know the names of all the patrol dogs, at least a hundred in total, and it is always pleasing to another driver if you are familiar with the names of his team. I think of the names of this particular team as I walk past: Tuborg, Frost, Lady, Fims, Børve, Snoopy, Buster, Tilley and Brownie. They are all good strong dogs, but of course not as good as my own, in my eyes!

Now I get to my own team, the dogs tethered on two lines either side of a tiny stream where they can get water to drink when they want. Having shared their company during a six month sledge trip, day in and day out, I know each one intimately; I know their temperaments and personalities in just the same way as the people I have sledged with. The dogs are all jumping wildly in the air; they are so glad to see me as I take a walk around. Most will jump right into my arms but there are a few who are a little more reserved. I spend a few minutes with each dog, playing around, checking that the everything is OK, that the water is within reach and that the collar is not chafing. While we talk together, the dog is ecstatic and licks my face and generally gives me a great welcome. When I have to move on to the next one, it looks sad for a few moments and then joins in the general clamour with all the others and snarls furiously at its neighbour on the other side.

Once I have been through my whole team, I carry on with my

walk and everything falls quiet behind me. I pass the slipway where the boats can be drawn up out of the water. Only one, *Agsut* (meaning 'fast'), is there today, while *Imaqa* ('maybe') is away on a depot trip with its crew and will not be back until later tomorrow. Walking on, there is a myriad of small yellow flowers lining either side of the gravel track. This brings me down to Sandodden, the old station first built in 1922 as a trappers home and then used by Sirius until the present station was built. It is only a tiny hut by modern standards and must have been cosy to live in.

Finally, I reach the disused weather station, painted in the characteristic light green colours of the GTO (Greenland Technical Organisation). The paint is peeling off here and there but apart from that the station is just as it was when closed down in 1975. It is like a small ghost town. The three tall aerial masts, used for sending weather reports to the outside world every three hours, are now silent. They will stand as a landmark by the dead station and a reminder of past times until, one day, a storm will no doubt bring them down. There are other such buildings further along these shores, telling the same sad story; they have become redundant thanks to technical developments and budgetary cutbacks. Automatic weather stations now do the job that men once did.

Luckily, from my point of view, technology has not yet devised a viable alternative to the sledge dog and sledge yet, and on this encouraging thought, I head back towards Sirihus.

Entering the yard, a couple of eight-week-old puppies stop their pretend fighting and run over to me. Their mother, who is lying by the kennel, watches them with some concern and yelps anxiously; the puppies continue to ignore her and carry on running towards me with their ears flopping up and down. I sit down on the ground and they run over me with legs, bodies and tails flailing everywhere. I play with them for a while and then go over to the mother who is still whining anxiously, while the puppies play wildly around my legs. The bitch is looking at me with shy and beseeching eyes which half close with pleasure as I scratch her neck. She doesn't look as though she cares all that much that her badly-behaved babies are tearing my trouser legs to shreds.

One of the Sirius men comes from the Lower House and we walk together over to Sirihus. While he has his fried eggs and I am drinking a coffee, we talk about the dogs. "How is it going with Duppen (the Boss); is he fit?" he asks.

"Oh yes, he is as fresh as a sea eagle again," I answer, and remember how close I came to losing him, the biggest and best dog in my team, through an accident one Sunday about a month ago.

That day, four of us had decided to walk about eight km in to Kuppelpasset to look at some ice caves worn by the river. Partly for the company and partly for the exercise, we each took one of our dogs along and enjoyed ourselves as we were walking at a leisurely pace, enjoying the peace. The dogs, as always, had plenty to see to, running to and fro, sniffing and lifting a leg every other second.

It was 1 July; a lovely time of year. The snow was melting at its maximum rate and the birds were singing. We were quite warm in shirtsleeves.

About half way to Kuppelpasset, we saw a couple of muskoxen grazing some distance away. The dogs immediately ran ahead to bark at them and the muskoxen were so surprised that they seemed to forget to run off. Instead they stood close together, forming a so-called karré, and lowered their heads warningly in much the same way as, in the old wild-west films, wagons would be drawn up into a defensive ring with the Indians circling around. The muskoxen were attacked from both sides but only superficially, for neither party could really hurt the other. The dogs were fast and agile while the muskoxen had their massively solid foreheads and large sharp horns (plate three).

We were taking photographs from a safe distance and then decided to carry on with our walk and leave the muskoxen in peace. The dogs were enjoying the game and we had to shout sharply to get them to lay off and come with us.

We had almost reached the river at Kuppelpasset, when we ran into another muskox, a solitary bull. Before any of us had time to react, the dogs were running at full speed to meet their new 'playmate'. Unfortunately, things went rather differently this time. This muskox attacked at great speed and in their surprise, the dogs got in each other's way. One of the dogs, Duppen was, in the next instant, thrown several metres into the air and the furious muskox then tried to gore him with one of his massive horns. We watched, stunned. The other dogs started to retreat; this was a tough playmate. Duppen was left lying there for several moments, as if dead, before staggering to his feet and making good his escape.

"Thank God," I thought: "You have learnt a lesson there, boy," but as soon as Duppen reached safer ground, he began to stagger and a moment later collapsed at my feet whimpering with pain. What on earth had happened to him? We bent over and could see that he had a five centimetre long wound in the chest behind his left foreleg. We could see all the way in to his lung. It looked very serious and we had to make a fast decision because the angrily snorting muskox was approaching. We had a weapon ready but we certainly didn't want to have to do any killing or wounding. In the meantime, I was trying to get Duppen on his feet although his complaining squeals got louder and louder.

The others looked enquiringly at me; they knew as well as I did that, without a stretcher, it would be impossible to carry an injured dog weighing 45 kg back to the station and that it would take at least two hours just to go back to get a stretcher. That would be too late if the bleeding continued at its present rapid rate.

It tore at my heart to hear the dog screaming. I must find a way to help, and quickly, or else end his suffering. I began to take my pistol out of its holster but no, there must be another way. Duppen was a great dog and there had to be a way to save him.

"Does anyone have a plastic bag?" I asked as I began to take off my belt. I examined the wound and could not see any air bubbles. Good, so the lung may not be punctured. While one of us held the plastic bag over the wound, I put my belt round his chest to hold the bag in place in an attempt to reduce the bleeding. Duppen had calmed down a bit and was just whimpering; it had probably been fear that made him scream so, but would he get up again?

We gathered our things together and went a few metres away. When I called to him, Duppen staggered to his feet and limped towards me with his head bowed down. I made a fuss of him and began to feel a little more optimistic but the question now was, would he manage to walk the eight km back to the station.

He did. It was a long, long walk for Duppen and the whole way was marked by drops of his blood. All the time, we were calling him and encouraging him to keep him going; often he stopped just to gather some more strength. For the last half kilometre, he was staggering like a drunk, but as soon as we got back to the dog kennels, the Dog Man got ready with all the medical gear.

The easiest part was to get Duppen to lie down; he just spread himself out on the floor. Then he had to be anaesthetised, preferably with a local anaesthetic using freezer spray only, but each time we touched the wound, he began to howl and scream again. There was nothing for it but to make him completely unconscious and that meant morphine from the medicine cabinet. We gave him a shot and he was soon sleeping deeply. The Dog Man could start to clean the wound and shave around it. For at least an hour, he worked away with sterile forceps, needles and things that must not be touched by hand, stitching the dog's skin that seemed to behave like rubber. At last the wound was closed and, though some of the workmanship may not have been exactly as the text book prescribed for an examination, it worked.

During the operation, all the Sirius men had been waiting outside the kennels; they knew well what the loss of one of the best dogs would mean, but Duppen was still alive and was carried, all bandaged up, into the room that was used for whelping. Two hours later he recovered consciousness, though he looked tired — but then who wouldn't?

The next morning, I went down to look at the patient and to my surprise he was walking round the room and wagging his tail as though there was nothing wrong. In the days that followed, we had only to change the dressings regularly and treat the wound with penicillin powder.

This accident to Duppen happened only a short time before I and my comrades were flown off on our traditional summer holiday visit to Iceland. We were only away for six days and as we landed back at Kap Berghaus (Daneborg), one of the Sirius men told me that Duppen was about to die. Naturally, I hurried over to see him and if he wasn't actually dying he was certainly barely recognisable. He had been a large dog before all the trouble, but now he was enormous; like an airship.

I don't know what had happened, but Duppen's body had somehow become filled with air; there was no sign that he was dying because he came to greet me and dance around me just as he always used to. There seemed to be nothing that we could do, other than wait and see what developed.

On the journey back from Iceland, we had the company of the Sirius doctor, Leif Vanggaard, who came to me the following day, quite excited, and asked if it was my dog, the big black one down by the fjord. Yes, I said, but why?

"I am afraid that his condition is serious, because his left eye has become white and milky-looking."

I was able to smile and tell Vanggaard that Duppen's eye had been that way since he was a puppy when it had been injured in a fight. Everything turned out well in the end and Duppen returned to his normal size and eventually to sledging again. He was one of the very best.

While I have been sitting here and letting my thoughts wander, I have finished my cup of coffee and my companion asks if we are still going to take a walk to Kap Berghaus to look for walrus. It seems like a good idea, so we collect our camera gear and get going.

When we reach the cape it looks as though our luck is out; a seemingly empty beach is all that lies in front of us. A pity; the walruses were seen here the previous evening, but where are they now? Ah, just a minute; those are rather unusual looking stones over there ... so, the walruses are still around.

We get our cameras ready and creep stealthily towards the animals. Stealth proves to be unnecessary when we see that they are fast asleep and snoring in the warm sun. We even have to make a noise in the gravel to wake them and get some action. One of the four male monsters wakes up first, lifts his head with the long tusks and looks at us with watery eyes, before letting out a grunt which produces a cloud of steam and a trickle of slime from its nose. This wakes the others and, in the next moment, a couple of tons of animal is moving inelegantly, but with surprising speed towards the water where it can swim around in safety. About two hundred metres out, they stop and watch our movements along the beach, apparently anxious to get back and resume their sunbathing.

Walking home along the shoreline, we find a pair of stranded jellyfish, which is surprising considering that the sea water is so cold. In fact, it is a constant source of surprise to us just how rich in wildlife this harsh area is and how unaffected the bird and animal populations are by our habitation nearby. Though only a small settlement, the station still smells of people and smoke; things that wildlife would normally be expected to avoid.

In the winter, there are often polar bears around as well. One of them even broke into our food store and smashed some of the freezers there before we chased it away. There is a limit to our hospitality!

In the dark of winter time, muskoxen have also been known to come into the area of the station to find patches of grass that may still not be covered by snow. They get so close that, on some occasions when it has been difficult to open the hut door, the obstruction has turned out to be not a big new snowdrift outside but a muskox leaning against it!

It is not only the large animals that are regular visitors to Daneborg; white arctic hares hop down from the mountains and ermine are seen from time to time near the dog kennels where they probably nest.

Ravens are constant guests throughout the year. They scavenge for food on the garbage pile and these large blue-black birds can often be seen perched on a mast or pole, watching everything that moves around the station. They can easily be mistaken for slow and clumsy birds but they are ingenious thieves and I have many times been fascinated to watch them taking food from the dogs.

As an example of how they manage this, one may see a pair of ravens walking slowly around a group of chained dogs. The birds get so confident that they approach ever closer to the tethered dogs until they seem only a hair's breadth from the gnashing teeth. They seem to know exactly how long the dog chain is and they ignore the dog totally even though it may be frantic with rage and frustration.

While a dog is thus occupied with trying to reach one of the ravens, the other bird will calmly steal any meat or dried fish scraps that it can; even whole dried fish. The dogs, I suppose, realise that they are being stitched up but, as soon as they turn to catch one thief, the other will nip in to the ring and the dog finds itself snapping at empty space, so fast do the birds move. One can feel quite sorry for the dog; the ravens play a kind of ping-pong with it. Sometimes a single raven will play the same game by sitting and watching until it can see that one dog is asleep or maybe having a quarrel and snarling at a neighbour. Once it is sure, it will fly silently round behind the luckless animal and, without a sound, land and take some food.

A lot of migrant birds can be seen around the station during the summer months. Commonest and most striking of these is the eider duck which, in an interesting way, has learnt to make its own use of the station and those who live there, especially the dogs.

The eider ducks nest in colonies and, in earlier times, one of their favourite colony locations was Sandøen, a small sand bank in Young Sund near to Kap Berghaus. At some stage the birds must have begun to fly to Daneborg to breed and, amazingly, started to build their nests (with their extremely fine feathers) close by the sledge dogs. In the mid 1950s there were only a couple of pairs or so but the rumours of good nesting conditions must have spread, and every year the colony at Daneborg grew in size until, in the end, Sandøen was left to the terns and other birds at breeding time.

The questions of why the birds choose to nest on Sandøen and other small islands and why the eiders moved in to Daneborg are probably answered quite simply by considering their safety from their greatest enemy, the arctic fox who likes very much to vary his diet in the summer months by eating fresh bird's eggs. As the ice in Young Sund does not usually disappear until the middle of July there is, as a rule, unbroken ice out as far as Sandoen for the greater part of the eider's breeding season. At some point the birds must have decided to try moving their nesting place in among the station's dogs, whose presence keeps the arctic foxes well away, thus giving the ducks their own 'fox-free zone' for rearing their young.

Every year the eider colony is counted and as many birds as possible are ringed. The favourable conditions at Daneborg speak for themselves when, in the '70s, the numbers had increased to almost 1000 nests. It was unique to see this symbiosis between birds and dogs, but there was a price to pay and each year we would find that about 100 eiders had strayed too close to the dogs and been killed by them.

Back at the station from our walk to the walruses this Sunday morning, we judge from the music coming through the open windows that people are waking up. We separate and I go to my room to write a couple of letters, ready for a helicopter which is due to visit us on its way south in a couple of days.

Postal connections are a little different from those at home in that the collections are unscheduled and are made when opportunity permits. This may be quite frequently in the summer time; perhaps once or twice a month. For the rest of the year the mail may well have to wait several months, even half a year, before it can be sent south, but that is just one more facet of life at Daneborg which we have become accustomed to.

I have not been writing long when a couple of neighbours look in through the door and ask if I feel like taking a walk to Little Sødal. Yes, of course!

Soon the day is gone and, sitting round the dinner table, we talk about the day's events.

Some others have been on a boat trip across Young Sund to Djævlekløften. They also have encountered some walrus. The new Sirius man in the group was especially impressed by what he saw and used many rolls of film to record this odd animal which nature, by our standards at least, has not endowed with a particularly beautiful appearance. Those of us who have been with the patrol for a year, listen with pleasure to the newcomer's enthusiasm which bodes well for our mutual enjoyment of the coming winter.

Normally, the handyman for the day washes the dishes but on a Sunday it is customary to draw lots for the pleasure. Most do not relish the thought of washing up after dinner for twenty or so people and when the cook puts the dice on the table, conversation dries up. Once the decision has been made, there is laughter and banter again, especially so if the 'lucky' ones to wash up include Gulli or one of the summer helpers who take no part in the normal weekday washing and cooking chores.

In the end, the kitchen is usually full of Sirius men who all give a helping hand once the excitement of the dice is over, mostly so that they can continue their earlier, interrupted conversations.

Normally, everyone gathers later on for Sunday evening coffee. This means a lot in such a small society and helps to keep the whole team together and avoid the formation of cliques and groups which exclude others. At this evening coffee there is usually someone who turns up with pictures or a movie or some such entertainment; the mess is blacked out and while the person tells his story or shows his pictures of a sledge trip or depot trip or whatever, everyone else relaxes and listens and watches. These interludes can be very interesting if they concern somewhere one has been or may be going in the future, and they are a good chance to pick up information about all the different parts of the country, for future reference.

After the picture show, there is often a lively discussion. For the summer visitors who are not members of the patrol, these discussions can without doubt become really boring but, for the Sirius people, they often go on for many hours and involve all sorts of argument and discussion. Gulli, who has himself been a patrol man through a two-year period, likes to take part in these debates and yarn about what happened in earlier years. We enjoy seeing this new side to Gulli's character, so different to his manner at the training school but, when Gulli is at Daneborg, he is a Sirius member just like the rest of us, with the added bonus that he has the natural authority and extensive knowledge resulting from many years experience in the job.

Often we will sit and talk until late into the night; in fact, as long as there are people in the mess, strong coffee on the side and Three Nuns tobacco in Gulli's pipe. No-one has any regrets until the breakfast call over the intercom from the cook early the next morning.

3. AUTUMN

Autumn with Sirius

In the last days of August the harsh reality hits us that, all of a sudden, the summer is nearly over. The sun begins to dip behind the northern mountains at midnight, and the sunsets get more magnificent every evening. Often the sky seems to be on fire, with spectacular displays of colours ranging from orange-yellow through to reddish violet.

In a way, this period when the sun begins to set at night gives the feeling that time has stood still all summer but is now taking great leaps to catch up.

Soon the season changes fully into autumn, the summer disappears as suddenly as it appeared and from then on, it is only a matter of days before the ground is once more frozen as hard as iron.

The last of the migrating birds depart for the south, along with our summer workers and visitors who have been helping around the station during the summer months. A relaxing silence settles over Daneborg and we all take a deep breath as the last plane disappears into the southern sky. For the first time, the new Sirius men begin to appreciate just how cut off from home they now find themselves. It is a comfortable enough feeling; all the untidyness resulting from the summer's bustle and confusion can be cleaned up at last and preparations can go ahead for our main activity, the sledge patrols.

One of the most important features of Sirius is that it has been able to function continuously, without interruption, since it started in 1950. The corresponding wealth of experience that has accumulated year by year, has been passed on from one group to the next; from old hand to new member, and from one sledge partner to another. Sledge partner and sledge team are two words which are central to the Sirius organisation but what do these words really mean? The official explanation is this:

A sledge team is a unit with which Sirius carries out the patrols of its allotted territory. It consists of ten male dogs and one bitch, together with a fully loaded sledge, controlled by two men who are called sledgers. At least one of these two has a minimum of one year's experience of sledge driving and of arctic survival.

That is a theoretical definition, but the practice is a little different. A sledge team, in practice, consists of dogs, a sledge and two men of whom one is the leader (a second-year man) and the other is his apprentice; as we have already seen, the leader can be both younger and of a lower military rank than his apprentice.

From the moment that the sledge team is formed and for the following ten months, these two men will work together almost every day. For six to seven months of this time they will have to be in each other's company, whether they like it or not, for 24 hours a day, every day! For periods of up to two or three months, they will see absolutely no other humans at all; not one. For the same period, they will be totally cut off from mail, newspapers, radio and television.

It does not, therefore, come as a surprise that there is plenty of excitement among the patrol members when it comes to the decisions about who is going to be whose sledge partner. During the summer, everyone has got to know their new colleagues through working together and during conversations over the dinner table. They will have formed their own impressions of each other. I have already mentioned that Sirius men come from widely differing backgrounds and so, of course, there are bound to be those who have quite a lot in common with each other and also some less compatible, just as at home or school or anywhere else.

The constitution of the sledge partnerships is decided in much the same way as the selections at training school; each person compiles a wish-list which is submitted to the chief, in strictest confidence, and he then gives these wishes the widest possible consideration in deciding on the makeup of the sledging teams. It is not a simple task and there are certain practical considerations for the chief to take into account. For example, there are some personnel who can only do a short sledge journey because there must always be two people left behind at Daneborg to look after the station and maintain radio contact with the rest of the teams in the field. Two people spend the first half of the season doing this job and are then changed over with a second pair, out of the total of six pairs. It is only fair that a man does not have to do these base duties in both his seasons with Sirius but, at the same time, the chief must use pairs who complement each other. They must be capable of running all the equipment on the station and able to look after everything, work the radios and manage all the day-to-day chores, even when there are only the two of them. It is a gordian knot for the chief to reconcile all these needs with everyone's wishes, including his own, for he too will form part of a sledge team.

All of this may give the impression that life with Sirius is idyllically happy, but the relationship between Sirius members, especially sledge partners, does not always turn out to be quite as congenial as expected, even though all the personnel have been selected by, amongst others, expert psychologists. Why should incompatibilities become noticeable when special importance has been attached during selection to personal characteristics such as a high tolerance limit, good humour, and a balanced and helpful personality?

Let me, in my own way, try to explain. To start with, the relationships between men of the same year, who have all left Denmark together, mean a lot. For instance, in my own year, (1977-79 in Greenland), we had an extremely good team spirit and there was a great sense of camaraderie between us. Anyone could speak to anyone and we never had any serious disagreements, rivalries, or envy. It gave us an inner strength which each individual could draw on, if and when he needed encouragement.

It is, within Sirius, the second-year man's responsibility to see that everyone has a 'good, pleasant and enjoyable' over-wintering, and we agreed amongst ourselves that, when we in turn became the older year, we would not make it necessary to show ourselves off as the tough guys. This unfortunately is the label that some outsiders, and some Sirius members, have attached to patrol personnel.

It is normal procedure, within Sirius, for the older partner to decide on the sledge equipment and how the team is going to be worked in the field, simply because he has the greater experience and has responsibility for the safety of the team. Any reasonable old hand (and most of them are reasonable!) will, of course, take the new man into his confidence to build up the novice's ability and thus, also, his satisfaction with his work and the enjoyment of both of them. Unfortunately, this doesn't seem to work every year mainly, I think, due to the lack of self-confidence of some individuals. Because of this we worked hard to avoid such problems when we came to the autumn of '78 and we, in turn, were the old hands. I think all of my colleagues would agree with me that we had a tremendously enjoyable winter that year.

It is well known that winter darkness and the desolation can emphasise the worst aspects of some people's personality. Aggression becomes greater and tolerance decreases, so that even those who are, under normal conditions, very well balanced individuals can become very difficult to live with.

This is the less straightforward side of Sirius life. When I give lectures about Sirius, I am often asked: "Does it ever happen that sledge partners fall out with each other during a sledge journey, and what do you do then?"

Of course it happens; it would be surprising if it did not. Although it would seem to be easily avoidable, an alternative question might be: "Does it ever happen that two men who dislike each other, are sent out as sledge partners and if so, what happens then?"

In answer to the first question, even the very best of friends will have disagreements during a four or five month sledge journey. Almost all people will occasionally show aggression even under normal conditions and, on a long sledge journey, there is only one person to get angry with - one's partner; but that is as far as it goes.

As for the other question, the seemingly irrelevant one, cannot the chief take this into consideration and prevent it occurring? I myself have never been chief but I think it should be possible, in most circumstances, to avoid the risk of such a clash of personalities. There can be practical considerations (such as the station duties) that get in the way, but one thing is certain; one day in the middle of September, when the chief is sitting with all the names in front of him, he has to make these vital decisions and every patrol member has to have a partner. The puzzle has to be solved! I have certainly heard of some unhappy, or unlucky, partnerships that have occurred over the years, like loveless marriages; but, perhaps surprisingly, I have never heard of a sledge team that was unable to carry out its tasks simply because the two men could not work together. I think that outsiders, after some thought, may find this surprising, that two men can still carry out their tasks properly for several months, even when they are scarcely talking to each other; it does happen, but not often.

The comparison with a marriage is made with good reason, since there is a close parallel between a marriage and a Sirius sledging partnership. In both, the good and the bad times have to be taken as they come and handled in a mature and responsible way. At Sirius, however, the chief arranges the 'marriage' and his decision is final; there is no option of divorce. This has to be borne in mind by anyone when they first apply to become a Sirius member.

By the middle of September, once the sledge teams have been decided, final plans can be made for the season's sledge journeys and for the patrols to be undertaken. There is also a lot of work to be done at the station to make everything ready for the winter. Boats and vehicles must be cleaned and put away for the winter and all loose outdoor materials, such as timber, must be covered and tied down so it will not blow away or become buried and lost during winter storms. The sledge dogs must be moved from their summer spans around the small melt streams and re-sited closer to the houses. There they can be fed more easily; once there is enough snow for them to eat they will, of course, not need water.

It is also the end of freedom for the half-grown puppies who have, until now, been free to run around the station. They must be put on chains like the adult dogs; a change they heartily dislike at first but, after two or three days of expressing their feelings of misery by howling endlessly, they settle down and accept their new life.

At this time of year, when the days are getting rapidly shorter, a lot of things are happening around the station. The cook, the handymen and the radio operators have their regular duties, but the whole focus of the work is, first and foremost, on the forthcoming sledge journeys.

The day after the sledge teams are decided, each old hand takes his new sledge partner out on a local trip, so that they can see what is needed for their team. In this way they spend time with their dog team and begin the process of the new hand getting to know the dogs and how to drive them.

The old hand will probably perform the introductions by saying: "Here you see the best dog team in the whole of Northeast Greenland."

The new man is impressed and will try to remember each dog's name as it is given to him, which is not as easy as it sounds even though some are white, some are black and some are mixed colours. The old hand may boast, for instance, that by the end his first sledge journey, he could recognise every single dog at a distance of ten metres, even in the winter darkness.

This is actually not as exaggerated as it sounds; after looking at the dogs out in front of the sledge day after day, for hours at a time, one can believe the man who said: "I have looked so long at the backs of the dogs that I can recognise each one by the wrinkles around its arsehole!"

Each day gets colder than the one before and the weather is often unstable, with heavy clouds and a darkening sky. Soon the landscape is covered with a thin layer of snow from the first of the autumn storms. On calm days, a skin of ice starts to form on the cold waters of the fjord but the next day, if the wind blows from the north, the new ice will be broken up and blown away so that Young Sund becomes black once again with angry-looking open water.

The time for light clothing is past and the Icelandic sweaters and snow boots are brought into use. People come in at meal times with frozen blue noses and running eyes muttering such statements of the obvious as 'it is certainly cold out today.'

Over the dinner table, talk is all about sledges and sledge gear; trivial talk for anyone not involved but, for the Sirius men, a subject that can have life-saving importance. Everything must be in good working order and absolutely nothing must be left to chance when dealing with nature at its most unforgiving.

Words such as Nansen sledge, shear pin, and handlebar hang in the air, for there are few things in this world as important to a discussion between sledgers as how to design the perfect dog sledge, what type it should be and of what materials it and its accessories should be made. The same goes for all the sledging equipment; even the most insignificant details becoming the subject of hours of discussion and heated debate.

Since Sirius is a military unit, one might expect all these details to be decided by a higher authority and the appropriate orders given, but not so. On the contrary, people are encouraged to try out their own ideas and theories on important points as well as on minor details. In the course of time, these ideas will be rejected or adopted depending on whether or not they work well, but always the main objectives are to make a heavy load glide more easily and to make life safer and more enjoyable on a long journey.

I won't go into more detail on this except to say that, on one particular point, Sirius men are very focussed; that is the question of just how much equipment is really necessary on the sledge.

For safety reasons, there is obviously a minimum that must be carried for a patrol journey, for example emergency equipment and enough food; beyond that, it is very much down to each individual what extras he wants to take in order to make his life more comfortable. It all boils down to weight. The less weight a sledge is carrying, the easier it will move. Unfortunately, no-one has yet been able to work out just how much extra weight can be carried without making it appreciably more difficult to get the sledge to slide.

Any discussion on the subject, therefore, comes back to the question of where to draw the line. How many kilos, more or less, are important? Bear in mind too, that from time to time, the whole sledge load will have to be carried by hand over areas with too little snow or too many stones, the sledge itself being pulled across empty or even carried.

The whole question of weight divides sledgers into two distinct categories; the so-called 'weight fanatics' and 'the rest'. Let me take this opportunity to give a short description of just what I mean by a weight fanatic. He is a strange person whose common fate is to be grimly uncomfortable. He will endure most of his winter journey in half darkness because he thinks that a decent lamp for use in the tent will weigh altogether too much. In any case it burns a lot of fuel which will be much too heavy.

Others of this persuasion may return from months of sledging through superb scenery without having taken any pictures, on the grounds that a small camera with batteries and film weigh altogether too much to be justified.

Of course, one must give them their due, these weight fanatics but, when they go so far as to build their sledges with especially narrow runners and with bridges so low they almost touch the ground, then we, the rest, think they have gone too far. They make the sledge so small that there is not much room for the load and then they argue for hours whether to take one pair of woollen socks or two. They can be seen to go pale and turn away, when they hear of someone taking a small portable tape recorder to play a little music on rest days.

I will not labour the subject any further; it can become difficult for someone not involved, or for the weight fanatics for that matter, to see anything funny in it.

Day after day, work continues on the sledging gear and every time a new sledge stands ready outside the Syndicate, there is a small christening ceremony. Some of the sledge teams have a naming tradition, although there is a limit to the number of years my personal memories cover.

Sledge team number five used the colour red (each sledge team has its own colour for its equipment) and this led to sledge names such as *The Red Baron* and *The Scarlet Pimpernel*.

My team, which was sledge team two, used the Greenlandic name *Savik*, which means knife. So there was a *Savik*, *Savik II*, *Savik III* and my first partner and I, in the autumn of 1977, built *Savik IV*, just before the Syndicate burnt down. This excellent line could probably have continued for many years had not my new partner called his next sledge *Pink Floyd*! Self-irony is a useful characteristic for any Sirius man to have at his disposal, and it can often be seen in the names of sledges such as: *L'escargot* (the snail) and *Ra* (the name of Thor Heyerdahl's raft which eventually sank).

At the end of the day, nearly all the sledge equipment is hand-made and this means that it suits the individual's requirements exactly and also that the owner knows how to use it and how to repair it, often with only very primitive resources, if it breaks while in the field.

There are only one or two months for the completion of all this work and the renewal and repair of defective and worn-out sledge gear; a busy time at the workbench, the sewing machine and the welder. All the while, the snow depth around Daneborg is gradually increasing and the ice on the fjord becomes strong enough to withstand the storms; soon, it will be thick enough for sledge travel.

Training Tours

October is well under way, windy and snowy days alternate with fine calm weather and, if there is some fine weather around the middle of the month, a regular fever takes hold among patrol members. There is a rush to get started on the training tours, as they are called. These are the first, sometimes hurried, courses in sledge-driving of the new season.

On the first suitably fine day, everyone drops what they are doing and, at the dog spans, a crowd begins to gather. Some are dressed in their green patrol clothes and mean business, but others are just watchers armed to the teeth with elaborate camera equipment; there is usually something to laugh or to cry about which is worth recording for posterity.

The frosty air is full of the noise of excited dogs. They know very well what is going on when they see two men coming towards them with an empty sledge. No wonder the dogs are excited; they have had a very boring time for the past four months, tethered to their spans where the only excitement, apart from the daily feed time, has been to taunt a neighbouring dog.

When the sledge is ready and anchored to a post to prevent any premature start, the five to six metre long rope traces are laid out in a fan on the ground. Next, the newly made hand-sewn harnesses are put on the dogs and the new Sirius men begin to appreciate some of the difficulties. The problem is that one is dealing with real, live and very strong dogs. The old hand manages with an easy routine, standing over the excited animal and gripping it with his knees while he puts the harness over the dog's head, lifting the forelegs one at a time and pushing them through the leg loops; all done in less than 15 seconds. However, the new hand is lucky if he can harness a single dog before his partner has finished the rest of the team. Once the whole team is in harness, the dogs are ready to be hitched to the front of the sledge.

"Now you can release them one at a time," shouts the old hand, as he places himself at the front of the sledge.

The new man is surprised; he had not realised that after such a long break the dogs would still know where to go to, but as soon as one dog is released it runs straight to the old hand and lies down in its correct place, taking no notice of all the other dogs barking with envy. It wags its tail with excitement as the old hand clips its harness to the sledge trace.

Soon a fan of dogs is spread out in front of the old hand. There is some snapping and snarling here and there. It is seldom quiet on this first occasion when the dogs have been chained up for so long and thus unable to settle their irritations with each other. Now that the dogs are side by side, the situation, if it is allowed to get out of control, can very quickly develop into a serious and deadly fight. In readiness for this, the old hand has armed himself with the *Red Worm*, a half-metre-long rubber pipe. If his shouted threats do not have the desired effect, he will have to assert his authority with the help of the *Red Worm.*

While the old hand watches the dogs like a hawk, the new hand is told to get on the sledge and hold on really tight. Without taking his eyes off the dogs for a second, the old hand walks back and sits on the front of the sledge before giving his partner the word to untie the rope securing the sledge to the post. While all around the cameras are rolling, he gives the dogs the signal they have been longing for: "OK dogs, let's go!" The whole team, which has been poised with every muscle tensed for this moment, spring with their legs and, with a violent jerk, the sledge takes off like a rocket.

On this first start, the next few seconds are critical. The dogs' eagerness to run can so easily be overcome by their eagerness to fight and, if a fight should develop, the sledge is no longer safely anchored, making it extremely difficult to separate the snarling and biting mass of animals. As a rule, however, the dogs forget all their old quarrels and hurtle at suicidal speed down the slope to the fjord. The driver has to use every ounce of his strength to hold on to the sledge and he keeps his fingers crossed that the team does not divide and go either side of one of the large boulders on the beach. Miraculously, the teams nearly always manage to reach the fjord ice in one piece and the right way up; the dogs can then run as fast as they wish for a quarter of an hour or so, until some of their energy has burnt off. A couple of minutes is more normal, and the speed then drops off as the dogs slow to a more sedate run; their condition is not what it was four months ago and some of them have become quite fat, as have the old Sirius hands.

To start with, all this can look quite chaotic and the dogs will want to sniff around at all the scents and say hello to their mates as they run. On the sledge, the drivers can relax a little, laughing like kids. The new hand can, for the first time, take pleasure in becoming one of the select few to savour the experience of being pulled along by a bunch of half-wild sledge dogs in Northeast Greenland. It gives an exhilarating feeling of freedom. Not surprisingly, in these first moments, one thinks of how one has come to this christening in dog sledging and of the many hours, days and months since one first decided to try it.

The old hand is concentrating on the dogs. It is the first time he has had to manage them and, in these early days, it can become a battle of wills between him and the pack out in front of the sledge. The dogs must learn to accept the driver and understand that it is the driver who decides where they will go, and when.

Every sledger has his own opinion on how to train a team of sledge dogs and as a rule, it is unwise to try to tell an old hand how to go about it. In outline, though, this training can go roughly as follows.

For the first day, the dogs are given their heads to run at full stretch and enjoy their new-found freedom - within reasonable limits. The next day sees the start of proper training. Danish is used for commands such as '*Veenstre*' (left) and 'Højre' (right) and the shouted command is accompanied by a crack of the whip out on the appropriate side (on the right to make the dogs go to the left). If everything goes well and if one has not hit oneself or one's partner in the neck with the eight metre long whip, the dogs will veer in the required direction, pushed across by the dog which is running on the outside and is therefore closest to the whip crack. After this has been repeated a good few times, the dogs will automatically veer in the direction indicated by the sound of the command. It doesn't take that long, because most of the team will have been sledging together in previous years.

The two commands sound quite different and in addition, '*Højre, Højre*' is shouted as a short sharp command in contrast to the long drawn out '*Veenstre*'. To stop, the driver calls a drawn out '*hoole*', a command which the dogs have an astonishingly quick ability to recognise after a few hours of hard going. It is as easy as that, in theory, but in practice it can take a long time for the trust to build up between man and dog.

In these October days, everyone is out with the teams as often as possible; at least every second day. The training runs last for several hours and, as a rule, it is teams of tired dogs that return to the station even though they have only had to pull the weight of the two Sirius men riding on the sledge. The dogs' breath becomes frozen around their muzzles and they pant hard, their long tongues hanging out, as they walk back to their places on the chain and wait for a well-deserved feed.

There can be situations where the camera-carrying watchers have some really good events to record, almost always thanks to the dogs going wild at the start. Things can happen so fast and so unexpectedly that even the most experienced photographers are sometimes unable to react quickly enough. It has happened, for instance, that on one of these mad early starts, the dogs, seemingly going well as they raced down towards the fjord, turned right around through 180 degrees and headed at full speed back to the station. The end result of this is usually the whole team crashing into a house or a pole. In the latter case, the dogs always manage to show an extremely well developed ability to run round the pole, the other dogs and themselves about 15 times in less than half a second. It also happened once that a team collided with a steel guy wire supporting an aerial mast, snapping it like sewing thread, even though it was as thick as a man's finger.

It is only in the first few days that such disasters occur and, from then on, dogs and men have normally got their act under better control. The paparazzi have to look elsewhere for their sensational pictures.

One of the unwritten rules of Sirius is that an active sledging dog will be no more than five years old. By this age, it is usually past its best for sledge-pulling and will be put down. This may seem a cruel policy and no-one could dislike it more than the Sirius men themselves, especially when they have to carry out the sentences. This is, of course, why the rule has been made, otherwise the patrol's sledge teams might come to contain a high proportion of old and tired dogs that no-one could bear to part with.

The regular replacement of the dogs means that there is a constant need to train new young ones to work in harness. As each team consists of 11 dogs, this means that there will be at least two or three puppies brought into each team every year.

During the training tours, the new puppies learn to become sledge dogs but, since the first one or two trips can be so wild, their introduction into the team usually waits for a couple of days until things have quietened down a little.

When a young dog has to take its first training trip, it will ride in the lap of the new Sirius hand until the team is well out onto the fjord, by which time the pace should have slowed a little. While running at a more reasonable speed, the puppy is put down on the ground the right way up and facing in the direction of travel. At this stage, it will have only one thought in its head and that is to catch up with the older dogs. For a while, it will run behind them until a gap appears in the fan where it can fit in. I have seen, in some cases, that a puppy's trace will become tight almost straight away. Brilliant; a new sledge dog is there in the making, and all that remains is to teach it the finer points.

Often, the puppies are kept running with a shorter trace for their first time out because they have enough to do just to follow the older dogs. After a while, they will be picked up and carried on the sledge again to allow them to get their breath back. They lie and pant at first, but soon regain their eagerness to take part; no healthy dog wants to ride on the sledge while it can see all the others waving their tails out in front.

The Puppies' Party

To judge from the title, this chapter might seem to be about the puppies celebrating their first sledge ride, but the puppies party is the occasion when the puppies are named by their drivers.

Sirius tries, all the time, to maintain a stock of good fresh sledge dogs. The Dog Man primarily takes care of this by planning a breeding programme from the stock-book which contains all the family trees and information on the origin of all the dogs which the patrol has had over the years.

Firstly and most importantly, inbreeding is avoided and new blood-stock is brought in from time to time from Thule district and elsewhere. Secondly, dogs with abnormally long hair are not used for breeding, as they can have a problem keeping their coats free from snow and dirt and are therefore more vulnerable in cold, snowy weather. Similarly, dogs with easily damaged pads are not bred. This is because the late spring time can often bring a coarsely crystalline type of snow due to alternating thaw and frost. This kind of snow surface can become very sharp, almost needle-like. Some dogs are able to withstand such conditions better than others and it is this useful characteristic that is encouraged through selective breeding.

Sirius men have a preference for large strong dogs which, together with a regular and adequate diet, means that the Sirius dog today is the largest and strongest in Greenland, with an average weight of 37 to 39 kg being the norm in a team consisting of animals between six months and five years old. (This has become even more pronounced in recent years; by the year 2000, this average weight has increased by at least five kilos). The typical Sirius dog is not a sprinter, since it is not used for sport racing. On the contrary, its build is a reflection of the sledge patrol's need to be able to travel 25 to 40 km per day, six days per week and for periods of up to four and a half months. This travelling will be not just on sea ice or hard tracks but often in stony areas with poor snow cover and through trackless mountain country where the sledge must be hauled forward a metre at a time. Considering that the sledge loads will be between 350 and 550 kg, it is clear that the Sirius dog has become a remarkable draft animal.

In the summertime, when the puppies are running freely around the station, it is common to see someone pausing in his work to watch the puppies at play. In itself this is not so surprising because they can be very funny to watch, but there is another motive which is to see which of these small fat bundles of fur, on their wobbly legs, are beginning to show the best characteristics. Some are full of courage and will jump into a fight between larger companions, while others are more reticent and less courageous. What everyone wants is a puppy that is tough, good-natured and friendly to humans. Appearance is important too. I remember, for example, a bitch called *Snefnug* (Snowflake) who had four good puppies but the whole litter had the fault that their noses were pink; the pigs, as they became known, to the owner's enormous irritation. Even though they were excellent in all other respects, they were at the bottom of everyone's wish list.

As the summer draws to a close and the puppies grow up, each driver decides which he would like for his team and tells the Dog Man of his preferences; the Dog Man has to make the decisions.

Sledge dogs are the basis on which the patrol exists, so it is not surprising that there are old customs for deciding officially who has which puppies. Twice a year, at the beginning of October and in January, the traditional Puppies' Party is held. On the evening reserved for this important occasion, the Dog Man is host and, like the menu, which is fried eel, the programme of events is laid down by tradition.

When the last plate-full of fried eel has been set on the table and when everyone is seated, the Dog Man bangs the table with his ceremonial hammer and declares the meeting open. He announces how many puppies there are in total to be shared out between the sledge teams, then he re-tells his audience what the rules are, including the one which specifies that the national drink (schnapps) plays an important part in the proceedings.

Once this introduction is complete, the eels are started and the schnapps bottle comes out and, of course, the first toast is to the cook. One has barely taken the first sip before the Dog Man calls for attention and says that there is a job to be done and that the serious part of the meeting had better get started. He continues: "Sledge Team One has chosen their first puppy out of the bitch Bonnie; what shall the puppy be called?"

"He shall be named Knut," call the number ones.

"Then cheers for Knut, and good luck go with him in the future," proclaims the Dog Man and raises his glass.

Let me interrupt here with a few more words about the simple and quite serious rules which govern this christening ceremony.

The Dog Man, who is responsible for the puppies and the bitches on the station, now hands over ownership of, and responsibility for, the named puppy to the chosen sledge team. In this situation, it is both the right and the duty of the men concerned to drink the health of the new sledge dog and there is only one correct way to do this, as past Sirius men have decided, and that is with a brim-full glass of schnapps to be emptied in one gulp. Though this is a personal matter between the Dog Man and the sledge team, one would naturally not wish to withhold the right from the rest of the patrol members to wish their colleagues good luck with this fabulous puppy and express the fervent hope that it will bring honour to the sledge team, the patrol and their country.

Thus, it is not only permitted, but also welcomed, that all the Sirius men raise a glass and drink the health of the newly-named animal. In order to participate, one must do this in a decent and orderly manner and so, when the schnapps has passed round the table, everyone expects to see that the men on either side of him have emptied their glasses to the last drop and that they are not drinking anything weaker like beer; at least not until a decent interval has elapsed. If any of this procedure is contravened, there is an immediate and strict punishment that the sinner must drink a 'punishment schnapps'!

A moment after the Dog Man has disposed of the first puppy, he returns to the task in hand: "Gentlemen, the number two's have chosen a puppy from Jette; what will be the name of the puppy?" — and in this way the procedure continues through the sledge teams until all the puppies have been given away. Normally, this would be a total of between eight and 15; understandably, the excitement increases steadily. After the first three or four puppies, there are usually some of the men who say they wish to quit for a moment; but this will cause a lot of noise from the sledge team that will have the next puppy, who say; "Hey, this is too bad; we have drunk the health of your puppy, now you should do the same for ours!" There will be arguments to and fro but, usually, all glasses are raised, even though it is not actually forbidden to leave. Only the Dog Man has no choice. He must continue to the bitter end; it is part of the job.

It varies, as I said, from year to year how many puppies there are to be handed out. If, for example, the number is 15 then everyone is usually satisfied, enough alcohol has been consumed and the meeting can be closed without any great objections. However, if there should only be six or eight puppies, someone usually says: "Oh hell; should the puppies not have another name, a family name?"

"Of course they should," comes the reply and so there follows a formal giving of some, often quite peculiar, family names.

During this round there are usually one or two who excuse themselves and have to leave the meeting for one errand or another. The gathering diminishes until there are only a few left who continue to discuss stubbornly whether or not a decent sledge dog ought to have a middle name; in most cases this gets no further than talk.

It can hardly come as a surprise to anyone that these puppy parties tend to finish quite early in the evening; as reflected in a monologue on the winter's events written by some wit among the Sirius men and read at a later occasion. It declared: "The autumn's puppy party started as planned at 1900 hours, but the party took longer than expected and ended at 21.15!"

Perhaps some readers will be disappointed by such an apparently unworthy account, but let me finish the story of the puppy party, a story that cannot be omitted from any true account of life with Sirius, with a few less flippant words. I would not like to give the impression that such alcoholic goings on were too common. If anyone wishes to be critical of it, the criticism must be based on the correct facts. In my time with Sirius, the use of alcohol was as follows; none of us touched it at all for the six to eight months of the year when we were out on sledge trips or depot-laying voyages. There was usually not even any possibility to do so, unless we were passing one of our neighbouring stations, in which case we would be treated, of course, to the best of east coast hospitality. Here I am not thinking only of good food and drink, but also rooms, musical equipment and other personal effects that would be placed at our disposal without any question.

Apart from that, when we were at home at Daneborg, spirits were only served formally on special occasions such as the six major annual events;

Sunset party (4 November, at Daneborg);

Christmas Eve;

Christmas Dinner;

New Year's Eve;

Sunrise party, to celebrate the imminent return of the sun but before the patrol members set out from Daneborg on the spring journeys (the sun actually returns on 7 February at Daneborg);

Midsummer party, to celebrate everyone's return after the main sledge journeys.

On a normal day there would only be water or juice on the table, just as in a normal Danish home. There were, however, no restrictions on alcohol or rules about when it could be available. If a couple of people wanted a quiet nightcap one evening, there was always an open bar in the mess with unfinished bottles that the Provisions Man would have put out for a party or a Saturday dinner. One could take an Irish coffee or a cognac whenever one wanted. There was just one unwritten rule, that drinking had to be in the mess and not, under any circumstances, in the sleeping quarters.

Believe it if you can, but the autumn's puppy party actually had a dampening effect on the need for alcohol for some time afterwards.

Final preparations for the autumn journeys

A blinding snowstorm is raging over Daneborg.

It is an evening towards the end of October during my second autumn and I am sitting in my room getting the last of my sledging

1

2
SYNDIKATET

fn

4

5

8

10

14

equipment ready, glad to be indoors. The hut is shaking and making everything rattle, while outside, the visibility is so poor that one cannot even see the big searchlight by the Lower House only ten metres away. In these conditions, heaven and earth seem to have become one; there is heavy snowfall and, a moment ago, it was broadcast over the intercom that the wind was blowing at 70 to 80 knots. For the moment it doesn't worry us because a good snow cover that has been hardened by the wind makes a great surface for sledging; 'hardblown' as we call it.

When there is a brief let-up in the wind, I can hear music coming from the other side of the hut; my neighbours are also busy working. I am trying to decide how many changes of clothing to put in the plastic bags that will go into my sledge's clothes box. I must try to remember everything since, once Daneborg recedes into the distance behind us, I shall have only what is in my bag and it will have to last throughout the forthcoming journey.

One of our sewing machines is standing on the table where I have been modifying some of my clothing. I have put an extra pocket and a fur rim on my anorak, together with a few other details which I felt needed changing. Most of us have made minor alterations to our clothing to suit our individual tastes. One evening earlier in the autumn, there was even a fashion show in Sirihus.

It was the two men in charge of the clothing store who had the brilliant idea to show the choices available to us for use on the station and on sledge journeys. For a couple of evenings they had gone around looking very secretive about something so we knew that a plan was afoot, but it was not until we came to Sirihus for evening coffee that we found out what the Slop Chest men had in mind. The coffee tables had been arranged in a long line down the centre of the mess, with the arm chairs round about. We were asked to sit down while coffee was served and, after a little while came the announcement: "Northeast Greenland's most fashionable clothes store, The Slop Chest, has great pleasure in showing its range of the latest new models of arctic winter clothing".

This sounded good and in eager anticipation we sat down to see what would happen. With musical accompaniment, the show started and, while one of the men was dressed in his tuxedo as the master of ceremonies, the other showed one set of clothing after another as he paraded up and down on the coffee tables. We had great fun and I cannot begin to describe the fantastic outfits they had invented; besides showing us what was in the clothing store, the main idea was to have a good laugh. When there is no possibility of going to a cinema, theatre, or into town, it is invaluable for a good overwintering to have some people with the talent and the motivation to make their own entertainment from time to time.

"The patrolling orders have arrived!" comes suddenly over the intercom, a day or two later. "The radio operator will have the details in a minute."

There is noise out in the passage. People come out of their rooms, hurriedly pulling on over-clothing. The reason for all this excitement is that, at this stage, no-one knows where they and their partners are going to be patrolling in Northeast Greenland. We have been waiting excitedly for this moment for the last few days, because the radio telegrams with the details of our routes usually arrive one week or so before we have to leave Daneborg.

"Hey, what foul weather," is the call as we come into Sirihus. People arrive from the Lower House, brushing off the snow and changing to indoor shoes. Everyone has to use indoor shoes; it is required by the cleaners!

Gathering in the mess, we wait for the radio operator and the chief to arrive with the route instructions.

"OK, guys, here we have it." The chief comes in with a handful of papers on which all the sledge journeys are detailed. We look them over, anxiously.

I find the papers with sledge team number two's travel instructions and read hurriedly through the place names which will give us the clues to our route. Revet ... Loch Fyne..... Geologfjord... a southerly trip, I can see. Excellent! Last autumn

I was patrolling in the area north of Daneborg and am grateful for the change.

My new sledge partner is also the chief, Claus 'Tavsur' Birkbøll. He was a patrol man for the first time in 1973-75 and has now, after three years as Gulli's coordinator in Denmark, returned as Sirius Chief for the next two years. The nickname comes from his first spell as a Sirius man when, for the whole year, his split-new stereo equipment refused to function. It gave him the nickname 'Tavse', meaning silence, which in Icelandic became 'Tavsur'. To have an old hand such as myself, working together with an experienced sledger like the chief has both advantages and drawbacks. The main advantage is that he already knows the conditions and has learnt how to look after himself and his partner on the sledge journey. The problem is that he has already formed his own ideas about how the sledge team should work.

Fortunately, Tavsur was one of those people who does not push his own ideas and principles just for the sake of it and this was one of the main reasons we had such a good relationship during the ten months that we were together as a team. It soon became clear that we agreed on most things and on how jobs should best be done. From the start, Tavsur made it clear that although he was the chief of Sirius, for this journey, I was the chief of sledge team number two and he was the 'new hand'!

Tavsur approaches and asks: "Hey, Mikkel, are you happy with the orders?"

I am, and we move over to join the others beside the wall map and run a finger along our planned route. At the end of our own travel orders, it says that sledge team number two must wait at Mestersvig for the arrival of the Christmas flight. This means that, as we pass by Mestersvig airfield, we will wait until one of the military Hercules planes arrives on its annual Christmas journey. It lands at Mestersvig, before flying on northwards to make air-drops of the Christmas post at Daneborg and Danmarkshavn. We know that this flight usually takes place during the last full moon before Christmas, using the brightness of the moon to augment the weak midwinter twilight. We go and look at the calendar which shows us that full moon is on 14 December, later than we had hoped. This means that if the plane arrives on time, which depends very much on the weather, we are left with only ten days to complete our patrol back to Daneborg where we, together with all the others, hope to arrive by Christmas Eve.

We know that it is 300 km from Mestersvig to Daneborg in a straight line, so we shall definitely have to hope for a spell of good weather or our chances of getting back to Daneborg in time for Christmas Day will be minimal.

All around us, people are discussing their travel plans, questions and answers passing between the old hands; "Hey, how was the going in Dove Bugt last autumn, when you were there?"

The talk continues over coffee while, for a second day, the storm continues to shake the huts, but people don't hang around for long and soon hurry away to get on with their jobs or with writing more Christmas greetings. These, for families and friends in Denmark, will have to be sent with my team to Mestersvig so that they can be taken home to Denmark on the Christmas flight.

It feels strange to be sitting here in October writing 'Merry Christmas and Happy New Year', but the motive to write is stronger than at home where Christmas greetings can so easily be just a matter of picking up the telephone.

In the ensuing days, all our final preparations are completed and sledge partners sit together a lot as they go through the details of their routes. We can study journey reports from previous years to see how our predecessors have managed the critical bits and what the sledging was like. In this way, we can reckon up how long it will take to get from place to place. We look at where the depots are lying, how much they contain, and agree with other teams to take only our own share so that there will be enough supplies for everyone.

In this way, we come to November; the ice in the Northeast Greenland fjords is safe to travel on, in most areas at least. All is ready to start the autumn journeys.

4. The Autumn Journeys

Outdoors and Indoors

Daneborg is a hive of activity. Excited barking from the dogs mixes in the frosty air with shouting from one man to another, creating a noisy sound picture which is so characteristic of this particular day; the day when all six sledge teams set out in various directions to begin their patrol journeys.

It is a little before midday, with a grey dawn light; only in the direction of Kap Breusing to the south is there an orange-red glow to show that the sun is on its way above the horizon for one of its last appearances this year. For a short time, it will cast its sharp but powerless rays over the landscape and then, in a few more days, only the reddish gloaming will be left. This, in turn, will become weaker day by day; the dark time is coming to Northeast Greenland.

It is about twenty degrees or so below freezing as we carry equipment out to the sledges but nevertheless, we start to sweat. The gear weighs quite a lot, but loading doesn't take long as the sledge boxes have been packed in advance. Everything is already checked and counted, but we run through our mental checklists yet again to see if anything is forgotten.

Within twenty minutes, the sledges are ready, fully loaded, each one carrying everything that will be needed for two men and 11 dogs to survive in the arctic winter conditions. Two patrol men stand and watch the whole performance; the radio team. They must stay and man the station during the coming months until they are relieved. They will not have time to be bored. Every day they must receive the positions of the sledge teams and forward these to the military authorities in Denmark. As well as this, they must build their own new sledge and prepare their equipment but, right now, all they can do is stand with hands deep in their pockets and feel a little bit left out of all the fun. When all is ready, the radio man says: "Hey, I have made some fresh coffee, if anyone would like a last cup...?"

We all walk back to Sirihus together. Nothing much is said; everyone is still trying to think what they may have forgotten. It is also, in some ways, a time tinged with sadness for everyone. We are about to be separated from our comrades and from the cosy life at the station for several months. All the same, there is an urge to get going and soon everyone is outside again, pushing the sledges over towards the dogs. Wow, they really are heavy!

Hitching up the dogs is by now a well-established routine and, in a few minutes, we are ready to go. A quick handshake and a clap on the shoulder: "Goodbye until Christmas, and take good care of yourself."

The radio men stand by with a flare pistol ready to give us the signal to depart.

"Are you ready, partner?"

"Yes!"

"Then let's go."

We lift a hand in salute and shout: "Let's go dogs!" and, while we head down towards the fjord, a white signal flare rises into the sky. We fire an answering flare ourselves and then we are out on the fjord-ice. The autumn journey has begun.

From the moment the patrol journey begins, our lives move into a completely different world; another dimension. Times and dates, some of the most important parameters in modern industrialised society, become of much less importance. Our way of living and thinking changes. Almost without realising it, we become a part of the landscape. Life is lived in the present and is ruled almost entirely by the forces of nature and, in such a situation, the clock is not that much use to us. On a sledge journey we don't say: "We will be at this place by 1520 hours", but rather: "If the conditions don't get any worse and the weather holds up, we may get there this afternoon provided that the dogs keep going as well as they are now." 'If' and 'maybe' are two of the most important words, when travelling in the arctic!

When we have waved to our comrades one last time, Tavsur and I set a course for the inner part of Young Sund. According to our patrol instructions, we must start by visiting the fjords inside Clavering Ø, passing Zackenbergfjeld on the way, so our aim for today is to reach an old trapper's hut lying at the foot of this mountain; not such a long day at 22 km, but enough for a first day both for the dogs and for ourselves. Besides, the Zackenberg hut is spacious and in good condition.

It is great to be travelling again, feeling the skis glide under our feet. Four and a half months have passed since the last sledge journe and training trips have amounted to no more than sitting on the sledge and letting the dogs do all the running. Now, we have a more important type of load on the sledge and a lot more than just a two-hour tour. It would, in any case, be far too cold to ride on the sledge and take no exercise, so we ski alongside.

The conditions on Young Sund are perfect this year; just a couple of centimetres of new snow on top of the fjord ice; it could not be a better start.

Not many words pass between us while we are driving; just the occasional 'right, right' or 'left, left' if the dogs start to veer a little off course. The scarcity of words does not mean that there is something wrong; on the contrary, it is quite normal to talk very little during a day's journeying. The landscape and the dogs keep our thoughts occupied and, even if we are good partners and have lots to talk about, there will be plenty of time for talking in easier circumstances. Conversations are best kept for later when they can be made to last as long as possible.

We are making good speed today so we take a break at the halfway stage, just as the sun is coming up over the mountains on the southern horizon.

"*Hoole, hoole*!" The dogs slow down and stop.

"Lie down." The older dogs willingly obey but the two new recruits to our team, Soth and Clapton, have not yet learned to behave or to rest when they get the chance. I take the whip and crack it over their heads a few times so that they understand my meaning. The dogs have frost rime around their muzzles, but it is clear that they are not tired yet. A couple growl in a friendly way at each other, while others roll sensuously in the snow, following us with watchful eyes as we take off our skis and get our mugs and thermos flasks out of the sledge bag.

Steam rises from the hot tea and we are careful not to scald ourselves, but it is good to get something warm inside us. Turning around and looking back, our tracks disappear into the distance. Because we know exactly where to look, we can just make out the buildings back at Daneborg as small dark dots.

It is so quiet out here; the only sounds comes from the team as they move around making the clips on their harnesses clink, and from the snow which squeaks under our feet as we shuffle around to keep warm. We start to feel cold very quickly standing still, even though the weather is fine, so the empty mugs soon go back into the sledge bag and we take a quick walk round to have a talk with the dogs. This is something they always like, waving their tails and showing their pleasure when they get a bit of a hug. At the same time we check, as a matter of routine, that they do not have lumps of ice or melted snow sticking in their fur or in between the pads of their feet. Most dogs chew off such lumps themselves but a few seem to have difficulty with this and need a little help before the lumps cause sores.

Hurrying back to the sledge, we get our skis on again and, without hanging around any longer, continue on our way towards Zackenberg.

It really is an easy day. About three hours after leaving Daneborg, we arrive without any problems at the old trapper's hut. When we are still about a kilometre out, we shout in the traditional way: "Hut, hut, hut!" That alerts the dogs and we cover the remaining distance at a straight gallop. Just before reaching the tide crack (the shore line, where the floating fjord ice butts up against the land), I leave my normal place by the left handlebar of the sledge and run forward to lead the team. They follow close behind and, with no difficulty, pull the loaded sledge right up the beach so that we can park outside the hut door.

"Hoole; that was good."

The dogs know that this is clocking-off time and that soon they will be fed, so they are happy and carry their bushy tails high.

Our first task is to unclip them so that they can run around and enjoy themselves while we take our equipment off the sledge. The dogs love this free time after the day's work, when they can go where they like so long as they do not fight or make any other trouble.

We prepare to settle in for the night and I ask Tavsur if he will be 'indoors' man; on a sledge journey, the partners take it in turns to be indoors or outdoors man for a day at a time. There are certain routines attached to each job and, as we are going to stay this night in a hut instead of a tent, Tavsur goes straight in to light the stove and warm the place so that he can prepare some food for us.

At the same time, as outside man, I unload the sledge and carry what we need for the night up to the hut; such things as our sleeping bags, food box, cooking gear, radio and mukluks. (Mukluks are a type of long boot, originally a North American Indian design, with a thick insulated sole and soft knee-length legs).

"Which bunk will you have, Tavsur?" I ask, as I come in with the first sleeping bag; on sledge team two, it is the indoors man who gets the first choice. At Zackenberg, it doesn't much matter who gets which because there is more than one good bunk, but in other smaller huts it is not unusual for one of the bunks to be up underneath the roof where it can become extremely hot, or down on the floor where there is a freezing draught. Hence the custom as to who gets to choose.

Once I have carried in the rest of the gear, I leave the hut to Tavsur with his pots and kettles. Outside, I find the sledge chain and, while the dogs gather around me, I make one end fast to the sledge runner and pull the chain out along a snow drift where the dogs will be able to slake their thirst. There is no great depth of snow here so, to fix the other end of the chain, I take a steel stake together with the axe and hammer the stake well down into the frozen ground. To make sure it will stay, I go back to the sledge for the thermos flasks, take the tea that we haven't drunk and pour it over the stake. In a few moments, it is frozen completely solid. Now there is no danger that the dogs will pull it up during the night; in the morning, it will only be possible to loosen it with the axe.

Next, I hitch the dogs onto the chain in the same order as I want them on the sledge, with the wing dogs outermost. In this way they get used to having their own regular positions in the team. The dogs come obediently to my hand as I call their names; only the two puppies, who haven't yet learnt their names or the routine, have to be fetched. I take all the harnesses off as I clip the dogs to the chain by their collars. The harnesses, which have become sweaty, are already frozen hard and stiff. This is the most important reason that we always take them off. We think the dogs will be much more comfortable if they get a dry harness put on them before the next day's work and we know that they will suffer less from chafing which can greatly reduce their pulling power.

After all this, the dogs get their well-earned food which will be either pemmican or dried fish, together with an added ration of lard from time to time. Dried fish and lard are well known, but pemmican needs some explanation.

As with mukluks, it is the North American Indian who must take the credit for having invented this excellent travellers' food. Pemmican is the common name for a foodstuff that is nearest in feel and appearance to a large stock cube; a fatty, usually brownish substance. Its great advantage is its high content of protein compared to its weight. It is easy to prepare, as all it needs is added water followed by heating to make a porridgy stew. It can also be eaten raw, which is how the dogs get it, since its fat content is so high that it does not get too hard even at very low temperatures. The ingredients of pemmican vary from one manufacturer to another, but the main constituent besides fat is protein-rich pulverised meat.

At Sirius we have both dog and man versions of pemmican, but the only difference is in fact the packaging and, during my first spring sledge journey, I actually preferred to eat the dog pemmican, which was very rich in fat and also had in it some pieces of what looked like pork crackling. It is odd how one's tastes and needs change, for I have never normally had any liking for sweets and fats but at that time, when months of sledging had depleted our body stores of fat, I could think of nothing nicer than a large portion of glistening fat-rich dog pemmican!

While I am busy clipping all the dogs to the chain, they follow my movements closely and, as soon as I open the bag with the dog food in it, they begin to bark and whine ceaselessly so I hurry round giving each of them two blocks. They are unbelievably hungry and in a couple of large gulps, the pemmican disappears. Afterwards, they stand and look pleadingly at me as though I have forgotten to feed them. The two blocks are, however, sufficient. I have already checked the temperature, which is around minus 30°C and only when it gets colder than that, will the dogs will get an extra block as compensation for their increased energy needs and their greater loss of body heat.

Once each day we must send a position report to the radio operator at Daneborg, so I set up the radio antenna. While we are still so close, the orientation of the antenna is not too critical, but, when we are a long way away, it must be lined up in exactly the right direction.

Finally I can pack the sledge again for, even though it is fine weather now, there is no guarantee that it will not start to blow during the night; we cannot afford to have anything blown away at this stage of the journey.

I am just beginning to get cold so, moving quickly, I grab the dog harnesses and make my way to the hut. It is only half an hour since we stopped but in spite of that, the stove is burning nicely and the hut has become comfortably warm inside. Tavsur has changed out of his sweaty patrol clothes and has put on a thick blue cotton track-suit. In place of his ski boots, he has sheepskin kamiks (long-legged, soft boots) with mukluks over them. His sledging clothes are hanging to dry on ropes strung above the stove.

"Good evening," I greet him: "What kind of culinary speciality has the indoors man thought to serve up for his hungry partner?"

— a feeble joke since we both know exactly what the menu is every day. As a snack to start the evening with, one can of fish paste, one can of liver paste, four slices of rye bread, and a third of a jar of marmalade, all to be shared between the two of us. I hurry to get out of my sledge clothes and, since it is our first day together, I am interested to see if any of our habits differ greatly and in what way. The first difference shows up straight away. As I take off my cold ski boots, Tavsur comes and puts a mug of cold lemonade by my side. I look at him in surprise and he asks what is wrong.

"Nothing," I say; but I have become used to a mug of warm cocoa as the first drink, as my previous sledging partner had taught me.

"No, listen to me," answers Tavsur with conviction; "What you need first of all is a large drink of lemonade to slake your thirst; much better than greasy cocoa."

I can see the sense in what he is saying but, on the other hand, I like the cocoa to warm me up. We have to come to an agreement on this, because there is only a ration of one mug of cocoa each per day and it would not be very practical to prepare them separately. While I consider this important choice, which I shall have to live with for the next half year, I drink the lemonade and have to admit that the idea is not so bad after all.

I tell Tavsur that I agree with his suggestion and we have a long talk about how the daily routines differ between the various sledge teams and how strange it feels when something is suddenly changed. To an outsider, it may seem odd to focus on such small details but, on these sledge journeys, the daily routine is everything. It allows the certainty that one partner always knows exactly what the other is doing and that he is doing it in the way that they both understand and accept.

Outside, darkness is setting in, but Tavsur has lit a couple of hut lamps, and a Tilley lamp hangs over the table, giving a good bright light comparable to a 75 watt electric light bulb.

While we have been eating, it has become as hot as an oven and the chimney pipe is glowing red. Tavsur turns the draught control down a bit and after a while, things cool down to a more comfortable temperature.

I am just about finished with the outdoor jobs but I must write an entry in our logbook and radio in our position. Tavsur has to take care of the stove and the cooking, but this is not very time-consuming, so for the rest of the day we have nothing else which has to be done and we can pass the time in any way we like. Because of the constant work at Daneborg, we have had only very limited opportunity to get to know each other but, now that we are at the other extreme, it is not just myself who is interested to find out what common interests we have and what subjects we can find to talk about.

Once Tavsur has served the coffee and we have lit up our pipes, we start to talk, naturally enough, about our surroundings and it soon turns out that Tavsur is something of an expert on Zackenberg and the history of Northeast Greenland. For my part, I already know that Zackenberg is an old Danish trapping station used by trappers until about 1960. In summer time, it has one of Northeast Greenland's best salmon rivers running close by. Tavsur even knows the names of the trappers and can also relate the stories of a couple of expeditions that have had their base camps at this place (for example the British North Greenland Expedition, 1952-54).

It is a good subject to get started on, as local history has always been an interest for me. Tavsur knows a lot about it and is happy to relate it, so our conversation and the evening go very well and it suits us both that here, at least, is one subject on which the debate is unfinished.

Historically speaking, there is a special atmosphere surrounding many of these old trappers' stations. Zackenberg; Revet; Loch Fyne; Myggbukta; Hoelsbu and Mønstedhus, just to name a few, where Danish and Norwegian hunters lived in the early days. Even though none is now used for its original purpose, most of them are unchanged, standing as tiny wilderness museums; memorials to an earlier era. There is still some of the old trapping gear around, both inside and out, and some of the old kitchen gear can still be seen on the shelves. I am sure that the hunting folk would still feel at home if they were to return out of the past.

Even though we have many common interests to discuss, the desire to talk sometimes dries up for a while. There is also the possibility that one has nothing at all that one wishes to talk about with one's partner, apart from practical necessities. In both situations, but particularly the latter, it is a consolation to know that at least there will be great opportunities to use the time by reading.

When, in the summer, Sirius puts out fresh supplies to the travel depots, care is always taken to make sure that intellectual nourishment is provided in the form of books and magazines so that the Sirius men have something to dip into when the conversation dries up. It is in this way too that the trappers' huts can be seen as a kind of museum, since the books and magazines are never thrown out and to delve into old copies of *Uge Revyen* (The Weekly Revue) and *Se & Hør* (Look and Listen) from the '50s is to understand a little of how things were at that time. The same stories are there today, but with different characters.

It is always a wise precaution, on a long sledge journey, to have two or three extra books in the sledge box too. There can be few things worse than to be stuck in a tent for days on end, with a howling blizzard outside and all the reading material used up on the first day. If such a sad situation does occur, there will be plenty of time to philosophise about the state of the world! It is also a good plan to change the literature being carried on the sledge whenever the opportunity arises, but still, from time to time, bad luck strikes. This happened to me on my first spring journey when we passed a depot which had only a single book but one that I thought looked interesting. It would last until the next depot, or so I thought, optimistically. What happened? As in Murphy's Law, we ran directly into a three-day long blizzard and so I had to read John Steinbeck's *The Moon is Down* three times in a row!

It has to be said that these traveller's libraries contain an extraordinarily varied selection. Everything from *Bill & Ben* via Tolkien's *The Lord of the Rings* to a book where different researchers tried to analyse the historical accuracy of the Icelandic Sagas.

I used to stick to reading books for the most part but, on one occasion during my first spring journey, we arrived at a newly established depot in Danmark Fjord, and there were for some reason, only magazines, albeit a substantial pile of them. There was nothing I could do about this, so I started on a bundle of *The Family Journal*. To begin with, I read the various small articles but then I realised that there were eight to ten consecutive numbers. Hungry for reading matter, I buried myself in one of the serial stories. It was set in some fictional country estate owned by a dynamic and extremely wealthy heart surgeon who fell in love with the very beautiful, but chaste, serving girl (who was in truth the heiress to a financial empire); but he, until this and much more would be made clear in next week's number, could not have her because of her evil, evil stepmother, or something to that effect!

Well, I followed this demanding story as the events unfolded from magazine to magazine, but when I came to reach for the last instalment which, it was said, would, reveal the climax to the whole saga, there were no more in the pile. Goddamit! I have to confess that I had got rather carried away by this story of the *Silver Castle*, or whatever it was called. Desperately, but in vain, I searched the whole pile four times; it was not there. Disillusioned, I lay back on my mat and brooded on the unfairness of the world.

Time heals all wounds and almost a year later, when I had quite forgotten this tragic episode, I was sitting in a hut almost 1000 km from Danmark Fjord. By chance, my eye fell on a pile of magazines. Right there, on top, was a copy of *The Family Journal* and on the front cover I saw the words *Silver Castle*. Sure enough, I found out at last how the story ended; all such stories must have a happy ending!

There is another type of reading material in the huts which

can be at least as exciting and entertaining as the best novel, and that is the hut visitors' books. There is an old tradition behind the story of these hut books which goes back, in the case of Northeast Greenland, to the time when the country was first explored.

At that time, as now, there were certain risks attached to travelling in the Arctic so, in case the worst should happen and to give later travellers a chance to know what had become of them, the men would write messages. These would contain information on where they had been and where they were intending to go, on provisions, conditions and so on, and not least, in which direction any search parties should start looking for them or their remains. These messages would be left in an empty marmalade jar, a cartridge case, or whatever else was available to protect the paper from the weather. Such a small container would not readily be visible in such a vast landscape and so they would traditionally build a stone pillar, a cairn, in a conspicuous place which they could reckon that any later search party would pass within sight of. The message was left in this cairn.

As the country was opened up, hunting stations and huts were built at convenient locations, usually down by the fjords. Often the trappers were away alone from their huts for days on end to go round their trap lines and, whenever they visited one of the small huts, they would leave a short note with just a few lines, for exactly the same reason.

This tradition has lived on, in spite of the demise of the trapping industry, but today has more or less lost its original meaning thanks to the introduction of portable radio equipment. Sirius has, for its own purposes, changed the tradition a little. We no longer write about where we are planning to go because Sirius is after all a military unit, but apart from that, it is always exciting to read the hut books; they don't even have to be proper books, but can be just a sheaf of paper bleached by the sun. Here one can read about the sometimes dramatic conditions other sledge teams have experienced on arrival. Perhaps they have encountered bears or have come through a bad snow-storm.

Others may say how they have been out on the thin autumn ice or that it was an absolutely normal day.

It is amusing how one can often read between the lines and deduce the condition of the sledge team indirectly. Such a message might, for instance, announce tersely: "Arrived here from Halle hut in seven hours, in lousy weather and snow conditions. Best wishes, sledge team x."

Quite amusing, since it stands out a mile from such a terse message just what a lousy day it must have been. But, things can quickly take a turn for the better and, if one follows the same route to the next hut, one may read that the very same person has written five whole pages in an unequivocal declaration of love for Northeast Greenland, the wonderful sledge dogs, beautiful scenery and excellent travelling conditions. As I said earlier, on a sledge journey one lives in the present. One day everything is against you and the next, you may be winning!

Zackenberg has its hut book which we study during our visit before writing in our own greeting. We are so preoccupied with this, or something else, that I almost forget to turn up the radio at the agreed time when the radio operator at Daneborg will call: "Sirius calling sledge teams. Sirius calling sledge teams. Good evening, it is 4 November today..." After that, he will give the weather forecast for Daneborg and then call the sledge teams one by one to get their position reports. After ten minutes, he signs off and we can switch off the outside world and concentrate on dinner which consists of two cans of a ready-made meal and one can of fruit, to be divided between us.

At some stage during the evening, Tavsur asks me, with a sideways smile, if there isn't something about a nice warm, mug of cocoa, now? I say yes, please, and tell him that I get the message.

The sort of cocoa that we drink on these sledge travels is something that one can dream about longingly throughout the day. It is nectar of the gods for tired sledgers; thick and fatty and containing millions of calories, since it is made with sweetened condensed milk.

As the cocoa is being savoured, our eyelids start to droop and eventually we crawl into our sleeping bags. Tavsur finishes off the day by putting a good portion of coal on the stove, so that it will stay in until the next morning.

The harsh sound of the alarm clock brings me back to consciousness.

Where on earth am I?

Oh yes, now I remember. We are overnighting in a little traveller's hut, with the homely name of Grejsdalen (also the name of a well-known valley in Denmark), which lies by Kejser Franz Joseph Fjord. We arrived here yesterday evening after a 65 kilometre day and we have now been out on our journey from Daneborg for 14 days. Tavsur is indoors man; good, so I can stay in my bag until he has fired up the stove and has made breakfast ready. Only the tip of my nose is outside the sleeping bag but I can tell that the stove has gone out during the night because my nose is cold.

Tavsur has got up and has started to light the fire. He is clattering the stove rings and the shovel, so I give up any attempt to sleep again. It isn't long before there is a roaring in the stove pipe and a whiff of paraffin and coal reaches me. It comes home to me just how important fire is to us in this deep-frozen part of the world. If one could not finish a long cold day's travel by creeping into a tent or a hut and warming frozen toes, drying clothes and getting something warm to eat, there wouldn't be very much to smile about! Even though I am not looking, I know exactly what Tavsur is doing at the stove. Things must be done in the right way and with patience, even though it can be a damned cold wait. I remember my first encounter with a Northeast Greenland coal stove. It was on my first autumn journey, on a day when we arrived at Hochstetter hunting station; Nanok as it was sometimes called.

We had been one week on the trail, but it was the first time I had had the pleasure of being indoors man in a hut and, while my partner did the outside work, I had to light the stove and do the inside chores.

It was a fine example of the coal stove family, that one at Hochstetter; no doubt about it (plate 13). A big black monster with a baking oven and everything. In spite of my lack of experience, I was optimistic and everything had been left ready by the previous occupiers of the hut. They had followed punctiliously the unwritten, but very important rule concerning hut visitors which says that, when leaving a hut, the stove must be cleaned and emptied of ashes and coal. Fresh coal must be left beside the stove together with kindling wood that has been put ready, with paraffin nearby, so that the fire can be lit at once. Last but not least, matches must be left in the hut with some of the matches sticking half out through the lid of the box.

Why all this? If, one day, someone comes crawling into the hut with frozen fingers, perhaps having broken through thin sea-ice, only to find that the stove has first to be cleaned out and coal and sticks found outside in the snow, believe me, it is not just fingers that one is at risk of losing! Matches? One has to take the box between the palms of the hands and strike a match with the teeth! At Hochstetter everything stood ready, so I had only to light up.

I took a few pieces of kindling and put them into the stove and lit them. They burnt fine. Then there was just the coal to put on; no sooner thought than done and in a few moments I had put five large shovels full of coal into the stove. As the last lumps went in, the small flames flickered and died out. I tried to retrieve the situation by lighting a couple of thin pieces of wood and putting them in under the coal, but the only result was to make my fingers dirty and burnt at the same time.

Reluctantly, I came to the conclusion that I had used too little wood to start with. So I completely emptied the stove and began again, but this time with a good pile of kindling and, as soon as it began to burn, I put coal on again as best I could. As before, the flames died away and only a choking cloud of smoke came up from the coals. Dammit! ... I waited for ages. Oh shit! I have stood and fumbled here with this damned stove for ten minutes and my partner will soon come in frozen and hungry.

"Well, if you won't go with kindness, you will have to take some persuasion," I said to the stove, which answered by blinding me with more smoke. It made my eyes and nose smart. Resolutely I grabbed the bucket which I had emptied of wood, and poured a large dose of paraffin in on top of the coal, struck a match and dropped it in.

B - A - N - G !!!

There was one hell of an explosion, the whole hut shook and the windows rattled. At the same time a sheet of flame leapt out of this 200 kg cast-iron monster which, with all its doors and dampers blown wide open, lifted several inches off the floor while the coal, flue pipe and other bits and pieces hurtled like projectiles in all directions!

When everything was silent once again, I stood for a while and looked stupidly at the mess while dust and dirt settled about my ears. Gradually I realised that I was still alive but was just about kippered with the smoke that filled the hut. Coughing loudly, I staggered to the door and out into the fresh air.

"What in the world are you doing?" asked my partner as I stood there, black all over with soot.

"I was lighting the stove!"

"Then what are you doing out here?" he asked and continued to work while he muttered something or other about new Sirius hands and what he thought of them!

I can laugh at the memory now as I lie in my warm bag; luckily, at the time, it only cost me a big surprise and some extra work.

"It is pretty cold," says Tavsur who thinks that I am laughing at the sight of him standing there and stamping his feet by the stove.

"I am not laughing at you but, ... how is the weather looking?"

"Fine enough," he says, after peering out into the dark and, once the stove is burning, he hurries back to his own sleeping bag to wait for the hut to warm up a bit.

Half an hour later we get up and eat our breakfast of oatmeal with milk. Then we can lie back and doze luxuriously a little longer until nine o'clock, when the first pale light of dawn arrives outside. The working day gets under way and, as usual, we each have our set tasks. Tavsur fills our thermos flasks with boiling water and adds tea. We wash up the dishes in the rest of the water.

The hut is only about four square metres and feels quite crowded as we put our dried patrol clothes on again. It is warm too, which means that we must hurry to get dressed and move outside to cool off a little before we begin to sweat; sweating, as is well known, makes one more vulnerable to the cold.

Soon the dawn light is good enough for us to see, towards the south, the outline of Teufelschloss (Devil's Castle), one of the best known and most beautiful mountains in Northeast Greenland. It rears up out of the fjord and in the summer, is a fantastic sight with its multi-coloured rock layers.

I begin to get the sledge ready. The dogs, who have been lying curled up with their noses tucked into their tails, get up one by one, yawn and stretch themselves. A couple start to bark as they realise we are about to leave, voicing their impatience to get going. While I am loading my sleeping bag onto the sledge, one of the dogs throws its head back and starts a long wolf-like howl. Before it stops to draw breath, another one follows its example and soon the whole team has joined in, noses pointing to the sky, howling. It is a dogs' singsong.

It may not be to everyone's taste, of course, and to some it may sound a little scary, but it is music to the ears of a Sirius man because it means fresh and happy dogs for the day's travelling. The dogs only howl at this point in the day if they feel good. There are other mornings when they stay silent and an onlooker might be forgiven for thinking that the men have gone crazy (at last!) as one or other of them starts to howl like a wolf. This peculiar behaviour is not because they have spent too long in the wilderness with sledge dogs, but is to encourage the dogs to join in the concert. The men will then have achieved much the same as if they had managed to get a person to whistle on his way to work!

The day's howling lasts only for a few minutes. Tavsur comes out of the hut with the ashes from the stove and the garbage bucket. "They are in good humour again today," he shouts above the noise and carries on down to the fjord ice where he empties the garbage, pours a bit of paraffin over it and lights it. This rubbish is never left to be blown away by the wind.

Back into the hut to get my anorak and cap; everything is finished in there so, with the harnesses in my hand, I go back to the sledge and strap on my pistol. While Tavsur puts the shutters on the windows and door, I harness the dogs. In a few minutes, that is done and one of us is standing with the whip ready to control the dogs' impatience, while the other puts his skis on. A nod indicates that everything is set and we hardly need to say: "Yes, let's go" before the dogs lunge forward against their harnesses. Routinely, we look back over our shoulders to make sure we have not dropped or forgotten anything in the snow behind us.

There are large blocks of ice rafted up along the beach, broken and pushed up by the tide, but the dogs steer obediently between them with the left and right commands. They have learnt to steer together much better now that we have been on our journey for 14 days. With some hefty jumps and bumps, we are down onto the surface of Kejser Franz Joseph Fjord and get the dogs running on their correct course.

As soon as we are out on the fjord, we go through a routine check of our clothing and fingers and toes, which is vitally important in an arctic winter. This is easier said than done, for if the cold begins to get a hold of, for example, a toe, it will only hurt in the early stages. The toe will then go numb and is not so easily noticed, but this is an urgent danger signal; serious frostbite can be the result if the affected part does not quickly have its blood circulation restored. On a sledge journey, as long as we keep moving alongside the sledge we can, as a rule, keep warm. The danger is always much greater when standing or sitting still and then we must be constantly on guard.

Not all people are the same in their reaction to cold, whatever impression they may give. I remember one man who only seemed to put on his anorak occasionally, the rest of the time just wearing a knitted sweater with, on his hands, thin finger gloves. He must have had an unbelievably good circulation. Others, who were in no way fussy, always had to wear their anorak, mittens and hat. There are no general rules about how much clothing a person needs to keep warm.

Talking about frostbite and the means to prevent it, one's face is the area of the body most difficult to control because it takes quite lot of experience to know if you have lost any feeling there. The first tell-tale signs are waxy-looking white patches on the skin, and this can be treated by taking off a mitten and warming the affected place with the flat of the hand for about half a minute. The whiteness will, by then, have disappeared without leaving any trace, so long as the remedy has been applied in good time.

In calm weather, there is seldom any danger of frostbite to the face even at quite low temperatures but, if the wind gets up just a little when the temperature is below minus 30°C, the message must be 'watch out'. Among the first things a new man has to learn is regularly to check his partner's face when these extra-cold conditions occur. Sooner or later everyone, almost without exception, will get some experience of a frostbitten face. In the dark or in poor weather, it can be difficult or impossible to follow the rules but, after some practice it becomes instinctive to realise when parts of one's face are becoming numb before they get to the stage of being white and bloodless. Common and relatively minor injuries are usually to the ears and around the nostrils. Both these areas are exposed to the cold most of the time, simply because of their location, and they have a large surface area. The tips of the ears can easily wriggle out from inside a hat, and the area around the nose is made more vulnerable by the action of breathing. It is mainly the new men who suffer such frost damage through lack of experience and, perhaps, because they do not like to admit to being cold.

I got my first, and luckily my only, such frostbite on my first autumn journey. We had been travelling north for about 14 days, slowed down by bad weather and poor surfaces, and the dog food supply was almost exhausted as, one evening, we came to a little hut about 20 km south of Danmarkshavn. The next day was stormy and we were forced to lie up in the hope that it would improve. It did, at least a little bit, and as we had by now used the last of the dog food, we decided that the next morning we must push on to Danmarkshavn where there was a depot of fresh supplies. We also had at the back of our minds that the weather station at Danmarkshavn would be a much more comfortable place to hole up during a snowstorm, compared to this tiny hut with very little equipment and with bunks one on top of the other. The top bunk was only 40 cm below the roof which usually meant a bang on the head whenever one woke up after a short sleep. It also got extremely hot (about 50°C) up there because the stove had to be kept going so that the man in the bottom bunk did not freeze solid. Taking all things into consideration, no dog food, being frozen in one bunk or stewed with a headache in the other, we had no choice. However, we had not travelled far before the weather began to deteriorate again and, in the thick snow, we soon lost sight of landmarks and had difficulty maintaining the correct course. The wind direction was, as usual for such days, a head wind.

In order to hold the right course and encourage the dogs, one of us went ahead while the other stayed by the sledge to steer and to read the compass; no easy job since we had to keep detouring around ice lumps. A hand compass is not easy to use when one is moving, has large mittens on, and there is a blizzard of considerable strength blowing from dead ahead.

We made progress at a snail's pace and, since we had started late, it soon began to get dark. Reckoning our speed and distance travelled, we said to ourselves from time to time that we should get there soon. It became quite dark, but thoughts of shelter and a warm meal kept us going, with gritted teeth, into the blinding snow. For the last hour before we finally stood under the lights of the weather station I forgot, in my inexperience, to be watchful for frostbite. I found this out a little later when helpful folk from the weather station came out to give us a hand to span the dogs and feed them. They were not a little surprised that we were travelling in such weather but they asked us in, and the cooks soon had a warm meal and drink ready for us. It was good to be indoors, but I had not been seated for long when the skin on my face began to burn; it also didn't feel too good 'down south,' meaning in my crotch.

Once we had eaten, we were given rooms and had a bath so that we could get a much needed clean up. When I examined myself in the mirror, I could see that I had a long burnt strip from my chin down my neck, caused by the metal zipper on my anorak which had acted like a branding iron. There were also frost-nipped patches on my cheeks. The most unpleasant however, was in the crotch where frostbite developed the next day into an enormous blister on 'the most vulnerable place'. I don't need to name it and it was really unpleasant.

On my face, the red strips and patches soon turned into dry wounds. We had plenty of lotion in our first aid kit and it took only a couple of weeks for all the damage to heal without leaving any scars. I had learnt one of the lessons that most Sirius men learn the hard way before they can consider themselves trained in arctic survival techniques.

The only similarity between that day, when I got frostbitten, and now when Tavsur and I are on our way along Kejser Franz Joseph Fjord, is really the time of year; mid November.

Today, in contrast, it is a fine calm day and, even though the sun has said goodbye and thanks for this year, the sky does lighten a little around noon. We are about 400 km further south than Danmarkshavn and so, for a short while, the faint glow in the southern sky is a reminder that the sun has not forgotten us altogether; it soon disappears, leaving the sky once again dominated by shades of blue.

This blue colour, such as we see here in the autumn twilight, I have never seen anywhere else. It varies from pale blue in the south to dark blue in the north and it is a dark blue that is so deep and so clear that it is beyond my ability to describe it adequately.

I have passed many hours, on days when the going was good and the dogs staying on course without wandering off route, looking at this beautiful star-bright sky. Often at such a time I may see a small bright point of light which moves slowly across the sky, leaving behind a faint white streak; an aeroplane on its way between Europe and North America. I try to imagine the clean, washed passengers, comfortably seated and dozing now and again while smart stewardesses bustle around, serving cold drinks. Thinking about such things can make the fantasy go a little sour from time to time and, if it happens to be a bad day when things are not going too well, I could be forgiven for thinking; "What the hell am I doing here in this snowy wilderness, stinking of month-old sweat, paraffin and dogshit?"

Of course we can always, like the fox and the rowan berries, comfort ourselves with the thought that the poor folk up there in the plane are probably suffering a mass of every-day problems that we are spared. The house rent has gone up, the neighbours have bought a new car, the television has broken, the grass needs cutting, the wife is cross and so on.

"How long have we been going?" asks Tavsur. We have been on our way for some hours so I lean over the back of the sledge and find the map to compare it with the landscape around us.

"About 20 km," I answer and pass him the map which he examines for a few moments; nodding, he suggests a tea break.

We stop the dogs, take off our skis and zip up our anoraks to keep the warmth in. The tea is soon poured and we share a bar of chocolate which is part of our daily ration, giving us both a quick-acting source of energy. Looking at the map again, we can choose our target for the day's journey; a place where we can put up the tent for the night.

After some hours we get there. It is my turn to be indoors man so, while Tavsur lays out and fixes the dog chain, I unfold the tent. The tents that we use are specially made for Sirius and, like so much else, are made to the design proved by Sirius over many years of experience. I will pass over the finer details but will just mention that it is a tunnel type and made of strong cotton which is more resistant to fire and cold than synthetic material (see Appendix D).

When I have laid the tent out on the snow, Tavsur comes to help me put it up and then, while I crawl inside to put up the poles, he anchors the outside. Once it is up, he passes the things in to me and I arrange them inside where we will need them. These include the tent net which I hang up in the roof where we put our damp clothes for drying; the thick (three cm) insulating groundsheet which keeps our sleeping bags off the snow; the food box which, as well as containing our daily food ration, serves as eating, writing and working table; primus stoves that will keep us warm and cook the food, and finally the sleeping bags.

The sleeping bags are double thickness with an inner, an ordinary fibre-filled bag, and an outer bag which is specially designed. They are definitely not the type one would carry on a rucksack for an ordinary walking tour in the mountains. Each weighs 17 kg but must stand up to conditions that the ordinary hill walker would seldom, if ever, experience. Each is so big and thick that two people could survive an arctic storm inside it, if something went wrong and the tent or the other bag was lost. It is made to fit the tent and is strong enough to withstand the two years hard use that it will get during a Sirius man's two years of service.

When Tavsur has passed me these things, he puts the rest of the gear inside the tent door and then gets on with his outside jobs.

Everything we do to pitch the camp is pure routine. It proceeds in exactly the same way every day and works so well that neither of us needs to stand still, even for a second. It is important that the whole routine is finished as soon as possible because one must work without large mittens when erecting the tent. It is also critical that for the whole of this time, we must be on watch so that loose things do not get blown away. Every new Sirius hand would, for instance, get a very loud reminder from the old hand if he let the groundsheet lie loose on the ground, even for just a moment and even though it might be fine calm weather.

He must learn, from the outset, to do these jobs as though it was a dark night of blizzard.

To start with, I am concentrating on getting warmth and light in the tent. Both the primus stove and lamp need spirit to pre-warm them and, in the minute that that takes, I get on with other preparations. One becomes expert at doing four or five things at the same time. The track suits come out of the sleeping bags and are hung up in the tent net to warm. The day's food ration is taken out, and I begin to change my outer clothes. Light and warmth soon start to have a pleasant effect and I take in the two pots filled with snow for melting, that Tavsur has set inside the door ready to be put on the stoves.

In only a few minutes it is beautifully warm; I have got my cold feet into the lambswool kamiks and put on my tracksuit. My sledge gear is thrown up into the net to dry but, hold on, I think I have left some chocolate in a pocket and must get that out straight away or it will melt in the 50 degree temperature that will be generated in the top of the tent by the primus stoves on full power.

The snow in the pots melts quickly and from time to time, I reach out through the tent door for another snow lump off the pile that the outdoors man has left ready for me. When enough water is melted, I put the cans of fish and liver paste in one of them to thaw out. The water in the other pot I use for lemonade; we each have our favourite flavour versions of this drink.

Whilst I am mixing up the lemon drinks, Tavsur comes in through the sleeve door carrying the bunch of dog harnesses which are hung up to dry in their own place near the door; once they begin to thaw, it is nicer to have them there where the odour is a bit further away and any drips don't fall into our food!

Half an hour after our arrival, we can share out the tins of paste to spread on the rye bread and even if the menu is the same as usual, we enjoy every last morsel. Today it is Tavsur's turn to write in the sledge logbook and so, while I begin to find our dinner, he writes the usual notes about the day's events, the weather, the distance covered, wildlife seen and so on which, on our return to Daneborg, will be written in to a detailed report of our journey.

"What would you like for dinner, Tavsur; curried meat balls, meat cakes in gravy, or beef with onion?"

"Let's have curried meat balls and will you check this position for me?" he continues and passes me his map and scale ruler.

"One moment," I say and take out the cans. For myself, I have chosen the beef with onion; at least that is what it says on the can which also features a picture of a large juicy Danish beef steak with a big helping of golden fried onions. Inside the tin the reality is a little different, but I find five small frightened balls of meat hiding in one of the corners. That the balls are so small is hard to understand because they seem to have eaten all the onions!

I take the map that Tavsur passes me and check out the position that he has calculated for our camp; I get exactly the same answer, 73°14' N and 26°05' W, which looks about right. We always double check.

Once it is time for our radio contact, Tavsur tunes to the correct frequency. Radio conditions are not so good but we manage to make contact with another sledge team who want to talk to the chief, Tavsur. This doesn't go so well and all we hear are a few words drowned in a lot of static so, after a couple of unsuccessful tries, Tavsur has to ask the operator at Daneborg to relay the sledge team's message.

It turns out that they have been prevented from following their original route because of lack of snow in a narrow pass. They are therefore asking for a change in their route. We both know the pass in question and that it has a reputation for being bare of snow in the autumn. Tavsur writes a brief reply with new directions and sends the message to the sledge team, who can hear us alright even though we cannot hear them. Afterwards, we get to talk about this and how little snow there is in general this autumn. It is no joke for a team to have to travel over much snow-free ground. For us, though, it has been an advantage, with most of our route keeping us out on the fjord ice. On the whole we have been very lucky with our the surface and we have not encountered much trouble with ice blocks or with pressure ice because, for the most part, we have been travelling in the inner fjords. There haven't been any bad storms in this period, either, so the new ice has been able to thicken up without being smashed up into blocks and blown around.

These ice blocks, especially the ones formed in the autumn, give some of the most feared conditions for the new hands. (They are formed by the sea ice breaking up in storms and then re-freezing into a chaotic jumbled mass which can be horrendous to travel through; later in the winter, they may become partially or completely covered over with snow), Many new hands think that, after undergoing their ski training course in Norway, they know all there is to know about snow and ice, but it is one thing to ski in the lovely winter snow in Norway where there are tracks to follow; it is something else altogether to follow, or to lead, a dog team through these autumn ice blocks. Even at the best of times, to ski beside a dog sledge in Northeast Greenland is an art in its own right and I remember clearly my own first encounter with ice blocks.

It was on one day in November in my first autumn, when we were driving northwards up and over the isthmus at Haystack. We had stopped the dogs to have a look at the next stage ahead and, new hand as I was, I could scarcely believe my eyes; as far as I could see, the sea ice was smashed into what looked like broken glass on a very large scale. I thought it would be quite impassable for a dog sledge.

While we stood there on the beach, my partner got out his binoculars and studied the scene in detail. With my untrained eye I could see no difference throughout this mass of chaos that lay in front of us but, after some time, it seemed that he had found a way to go. We started and drove for some time along the beach before turning directly into the blocks. We struggled up and down and in and out over these polished lumps of ice and within five minutes I had managed to fall on my nose and the other end at least twenty times, as well as breaking one of my skis. Fortunately we carried two extra skis with us but it was a bit early to start using our reserves.

Often we met a dead end, had to turn the sledge around and go back a good distance to try to find a new way. This was really hard work and the sweat was pouring off me. It was also tough on the inexperienced puppies because they had not learned to keep their traces tight the whole time; any slack trace was liable to catch on a corner of ice and the puppy (or dog) would be stopped dead by a violent tug and then dragged backwards towards the sledge. Usually we managed to stop in time, but it was sometimes unavoidable that a puppy or a careless older dog would have a hard time. It was a wonder that none of the dogs was ever hurt seriously but, as I have said before, they are a tough breed. It is also something of a miracle that no Sirius people have suffered broken arms or legs in such conditions, thinking of all the splits and cracks that lie in wait for the unwary or the unlucky in that damned block-ice.

After some time, the blocks became so impassable that first I, and then my partner, took off our skis and went on foot. It was difficult enough to get through the blocks when able to hold onto the sledge handlebars, but it was much worse when the sledge got jammed and one had to balance on a tilted ice slab, step in between the dog's traces and lift the front of the 400 kg sledge single-handed. To lose a foothold meant, a moment later, lying all tangled up in the dog traces. At another moment, the dogs might manage to move the sledge by themselves without warning, necessitating a prodigious leap out of the way. Very few of us go through life with a burning ambition to be run over by a heavily loaded dog sledge.

After ten to 15 km and several hours of very hard tedious work, we reached the mouth of Bessels Fjord where the ice blocks became a little easier to negotiate. We were able to put on skis again and everything started to go more smoothly; even so, I managed to break another ski.

If, after energetic attempts at trying to stay balanced, one fell over and got left behind, the only solution was to get on one's feet again as soon as possible and try to get a hold of the ten metre length of rope that was always trailed behind the sledge for just such an emergency. Often it was only the very last inch that one was able to grasp but, at other times, one didn't quite make it and then the partner would have to stop the dogs and wait. He would not be happy about this, being inclined to forget his own beginner's troubles of the year before.

As time went by, stumbles became less and less frequent and one gradually learnt to regain one's balance, often demonstrating a degree of gymnastic agility that was truly amazing. How on earth did I manage to get on my feet after going backwards on one ski before falling more or less flat on my back? I wouldn't say that it makes an expert skier in the ordinary sense, to be a Sirius man, but one thing is certain; it teaches you to hold on tight, move your feet quickly and ... improvise!

It is a saying in the patrol that the chief purpose of the autumn journey is the training of personnel and dogs; a sort of general training, before the major spring sledge journey. Eventually, it all starts to hang together. In the autumn, one learns to judge the strength of the ice by its colour, to get a taste of the cold before it reaches its worst in February and March, and to learn the use of all the sledging gear. One also learns to control and move the skis by feel alone since later on, travelling will often be in the dark, or sometimes by moonlight if we can use the presence of the moon to augment the few hours of weak daylight.

Much of the time on these journeys, one is living in twilight and darkness and the impressions are vivid and unforgettable, especially in the autumn when one can, in unguarded moments, feel the full power, the terrifying emptiness of the polar lands. Most people know, I think, the melancholy that can affect them when the days are short and nature seems to have gone underground. One remembers the spring and summer and can scarcely believe that they will ever return. In the polar regions, these feelings are greatly increased and, on top of it all, there is the total silence.

This silence is a strange phenomenon. It is said, for example, that the old seafarers were more scared of the stillness of the doldrums than of the giant waves of the Southern Ocean, and that more eskimo kayakers have disappeared into the deep of a mirror-smooth fjord than in foaming waves.

There is something about silence that can make one doubt ... everything.

It is a peculiarity of some of these silent polar days and nights. Normally one would simply enjoy good weather without thinking further about it, but sometimes it feels different and one comes to realise this only when the moment is past.

For hour after hour, life is reduced to skiing silently alongside the sledge, moving mechanically in an almost hypnotic trance, walking and walking but seeming to get nowhere in the world because of the blankness of the landscape, the height of the mountains and the brilliant clarity of the air. These deceive one's sense of scale.

Quite suddenly, one's thoughts seem to vanish as though all ability to think has been stunned. It is alarming and scary the first time this happens, and one searches one's mind for something new to think about. No matter how determined the attempt, nothing rational materialises. Unwillingly, one withdraws further inside oneself into areas seldom visited of one's own free will, where thoughts and feelings flicker out of control. The surrounding landscape comes to seem as though it radiates an ice-cold hostility. All that one sees is this timeless eternity where one begins to doubt what is real and what is hallucination. Violent moods can begin to rage through one's brain as all ideas of time and space, reality and fantasy become mixed up and the over-riding feeling is of being microscopically small and lost in a dreamlike world. Yet, this maelstrom in the mind can stop just as suddenly as it begins, leaving a feeling of being eternally old and overwhelmed by a tiredness of life. Without rational thought or awareness of the outside world, one wanders like a sleep walker until wakened.

All this lasts perhaps for only for seconds — I don't know — then a creak from the sledge or a clink from the harnesses or the whining of a dog brings one back to consciousness and reality again. Maybe it is the sudden sound of wings or a hoarse screaming over one's head but, with senses returned to normal once more, there, high up, are a pair of night-black ravens. They croak again and one can follow them with the eyes until they have disappeared, before realising that there is no longer that overwhelming feeling of being lonely, old and afraid. As if re-born, one's mind is suffused with a feeling of limitless will and strength. There is the beautiful deep blue of the sky and the amazingly pristine beauty of the mountains. One hears again the breathing of the dogs, the harnesses rattling, the crisp sound of the snow and as a background to all this, nature's wonderful silence! Then comes the feeling of being in tune with the universe and loving life as never before because, out there in the great solitude, one has visited the borders of the mind and seen that only silence is great; everything else is weakness.

Northwards on a moonlit night

December comes and a weak twilight at around midday is all that is left of the day, as Tavsur and I arrive at Mestersvig, following our instructions to await the arrival of the Christmas flight.

At Mestersvig we are, as expected, treated with hospitality by the half-dozen airfield staff who have the task of keeping the two km length of the landing-strip open throughout the year. Not that there is much air traffic; perhaps only one flight every second month in winter time.

We have some great days while we wait for the flight but we long to get travelling again, knowing that a good 300 km of sledging still await us out there in the dark. Would snowstorms from the north hold us up? Will the Christmas flight arrive or will we, as has often happened before, be forced to wait for better weather? We no longer reckon that we can get back to Daneborg by Christmas Eve.

However, the weather gods smile on us and the plane arrives in the afternoon of 14 December; the two hours it stays at Mestersvig become a time of hectic activity. The acting coordinator, Jørn 'Tjock' Ladegård, has come up from Denmark to deliver courier mail for us and to take back our Christmas mail for friends and family. Hurriedly we exchange news with him and the last question has scarcely been answered before the plane's propellers begin to turn again. On his way into the plane Tjock stops suddenly: "I nearly forgot," he says with a large grin: "Here is something for your Christmas Eve in the tent. Happy Christmas, folks!"

Before we can give him an answer, he disappears inside the plane, leaving us each with a large Havanna cigar!

Once the aircraft is no more than a vanishing speck in the twilight, we exchange glances. These guys at the airstrip are already beginning to tease us over our lack of time, but there are still ten days marked on our calendar candle and the sledge stands loaded and ready to go.

That same evening, we leave Mestersvig as the full moon rises over the Scoresby Land mountains. We have waited intentionally for the moon to rise as, with only one week to go to midwinter, there is no doubt that where we are, to the north of latitude 72°N, the full moon is the brightest light in the sky.

Sledge driving by moonlight can, in clear weather, be an unforgettable experience. Myriads of snow crystals reflect the moon's cold rays and once the eyes have forgotten about electric lights, it feels almost as though the land is bathed in daylight.

What a landscape!

No ordinary words can describe it; the space, the distances and the silence are all essential components but greatest of all is the sensation of actually being a part, however minute and insignificant, of this huge landscape and of the whole universe. Undoubtedly one is marked for life on nights such as this, with time to ponder things and, for a while, question what is reality and what is truth.

As the hours pass and we sledge on beneath the flickering stars, our target, Kongeborgen, lies far distant in the moonlight but we are lucky and the travelling conditions across Kong Oscar Fjord are excellent. By two in the morning, after less than six hours travel, the mountain massif begins to loom larger ahead of us and the shadows and contours begin to stand out more clearly. This tells us that we are almost there, perhaps only a few kilometres from land. A little further and the broken ice near the shore appears; another quarter of an hour sees us at the end of our night's travel and we have made good 45 km.

Five days later, in the middle of the night, we are on the way up and over the pass at Østersletten. The moon has helped us a lot so far but its light is diminishing with each night that passes. A sharp freezing wind is blowing in our faces from the north, though paradoxically, we are pleased that it feels cold and fresh; as long as the temperature stays below minus 30°C, the wind is local and we know that there is nothing worse approaching.

It becomes a long night; we run into an area of thin snow cover and the sledge stops time after time on large stones. When that happens, one of us has to go out in front, navigating from snow patch to snow patch, with glances back every now and then to encourage the dogs and tell them when they really have to pull hardest. The other man, back by the sledge, is constantly watching out for large stones which are best avoided at all costs in case they break the sledge bridges. Every few moments, he will have to pull with all his strength on the steering rope and the handlebars. The sledge turns quickly and each time it avoids becoming stuck between two stones, a half minute of heavy lifting is saved. From time to time, there are sparks from the sledge runners as they pass over bare stones, but many times everything grinds to a halt. Then the sledge man must go up to the front of the runners, plant his feet firmly on the ground and heave the sledge free before leaping back and pushing with all his strength on the handlebars as he yells at the dogs, "Yes, let's go!" Our inner clothing becomes wet with sweat. Beards and hair become full of ice from our frozen breath.

We take a tea break before changing jobs and holding the steaming mugs between mittened hands while bending our backs against the wind, we look to the south. What a sight!

Like a giant flickering curtain, the northern lights hang in the sky above us. The olive-green and yellow colours look as though they are waving in a gentle breeze. Astonished, we watch in silence while their appearance constantly changes. One moment they light up in one direction and the next they die down and grow somewhere else in the sky.

We are often taken unawares by the northern lights in this way. Many nights they are not to be seen, with only stars and the moon lighting the sky. Then, all of a sudden, the aurora is there, sometimes as a large stationary patch of light not unlike what one can see on a winter evening over a large city when the street lights reflect on the clouds. On other nights, the aurora presents a dramatic storm-like scenery. Just such a wild untamed aurora I saw one December night the year before, as we were finding our way here and there down the smooth ice of Langelven. It waved over our heads from side to side like a banner in a gale. It seemed so violent that it made one stand and listen, expecting to hear the noise of a storm, but there was not a sound other than our own breathing; disconcerting, even though we knew, of course, that even the most dramatic aurora makes no sound.

We begin to freeze as we watch, and our body sweat is turning into an ice layer inside our anoraks.

Once we get over the pass at Østersletten there are only 20 km further to reach our objective but, out on the sea ice, we encounter broken blocks and it takes us another 11 hours of stumbling forward to reach our target. Many times we think the hut is in sight, but each time we fire a flare to give us some light in the darkness and it turns out to be a large square block about 50 metres ahead.

It is two tired men who finally let themselves into Knudshoved trapping station; the night wind burns like fire on our faces and eyes but nevertheless we are satisfied, for now it is only 70 km to go to Daneborg. We eat in silence with no strength left for anything else and we are asleep the instant we lie down in our bags. The last thing we hear is the gentle music from the stove; a mixture of the fire and the wind humming in the chimney, together with a small hiss each time a drip of melted ice from our clothes hits the stove and is turned into steam.

A day and a half later, on the evening of 21 December, we are ready to strike our camp out in Gael Hamkes Bugt. If all goes well this will be our eighth and last time of travelling at night this year. With such an optimistic thought, we decide to celebrate Christmas Eve in the tent. Besides our usual food ration, we can divide up the luxuries we have saved against the possibility that we will not make it home until after Christmas.

When we have eaten crackers with camembert and finished with waffles and vanilla ice, there remain the two big cigars that Tjock gave us. A quarter of an hour later it is almost impossible to see our hands in front of our faces inside the tent and, while we lie back luxuriously on the sleeping bags, we discuss how the autumn journey has turned out. We have to admit to being lucky. The weather, the dogs and the going have been excellent most of the time and we have been spared any serious accidents. We find paper and a pencil to work out some of the statistics.

When we have done the additions and divisions it turns out that, so long as we are able to reach home tonight, we have made an average day's travel of exactly 39.8 km with an average speed of 6.7 km *per* hour. We have covered a distance the same as that from Kruså (on the Danish border) to Milan, some 1300 km. The cigars taste even better with these figures in our heads.

It is totally dark as we strike camp, but after weeks of travel, the well-tried routine means that this is not a problem. Twenty minutes after we have turned off the primuses, we are ready to rope the sledge load and, at this exact moment, the waning half moon rises from the Greenland Sea to the east. It is a bewitching sight. One can really see the curve of the horizon and the moon is a reddish yellow crescent. We stop work for a moment and howl with pleasure in our best werewolf fashion; after a moment the dogs, one by one, join in our sing-song.

Four hours later, we can see the lights of Daneborg flickering a distant welcome, about ten km away. We stop the dogs for our last cup of tea. Lying with their ears pricked and looking intently towards the station, they can no doubt sense that the other dogs are not so far away. While we stand and watch, a couple of lights appear, blinking in our direction from out on the fjord. It can only be snow scooters. Over the radio we have heard that some of the other sledge teams have returned the previous night, so a pair of our friends must have decided to drive out to meet us.

We hasten to send up a flare and, moments later, there is an answer. The powerful light makes the dogs bark impatiently and as soon as we are ready, they leap forward. They do not look as though it is their eighth consecutive night of hard pulling. The lights approach quickly and soon two snow scooters roar past us, one on each side, turn around and then come more slowly up by the side of us.

We stop and greet each other in the dark, with laughter and handshakes.

"Welcome home, it is good to see you again," they say with a grin.

"Thank you, and you too. What kind of wild speed were you driving at, coming out here?"

"Wild speed? You yourselves have driven as if you had fire in your backsides."

We talk and smile happily. They have soda water and chocolate with them. Real friends!

"The cook has dinner ready at home," says one of our welcoming escorts.

"Then we must not keep him waiting, must we?"

An hour later, we reach the station where the other dog teams welcome us with a mighty din. The noise brings everyone out of the huts and again there is much shaking of hands. Many pairs of hands help and within five minutes the dogs have been fed with a large ration and the sledge has been unloaded. In Sirihus, a meal and two cold beers stand ready. The autumn journey is over and it feels good to be home.

5. Christmas and January

Christmas with Sirius

It is amazing how quickly one becomes used to living by the clock again after coming home from a sledge journey. There has been no chance to wash for weeks until now, all of a sudden, we can take a bath every day and once more eat at regular meal times as if nothing had happened.

The food can be a bit of a problem since most men lose between five and ten or even up to 20 kg of bodyweight on a sledge journey. Their excess fat layer disappears and what remains is a minimum for the body's needs. This means that we get accustomed to an almost constant feeling of hunger and, when food is plentiful once again, each meal is no sooner finished than we feel ready for the next. It is easy to get back to normal weight but, without care, very easy to exceed it by several kilos within the first 14 days. I myself have experienced a weight gain of seven kilos within the first week after returning from a sledge journey. It is so difficult, after living off tinned food and porridge, to say 'no' to a large juicy beef steak, fresh baked cakes, or rich cream. A snack at night can also quickly become a habit over Christmas time.

Christmases, as we celebrate them at Sirius are, however, among the happiest I have ever experienced. In the first place, the Christmas rush does not start until Christmas Eve, not counting the hurry to get home in time for it, and for a second thing, Christmas Eve has a more important meaning for people so far away from parents and family. On top of that, we are more than happy to surrender to the pleasure of eating.

In both my first and second years, the last sledge team to return to Daneborg got back on the afternoon of 24 December and on one occasion, this was the same sledge team that had to arrange the Christmas Eve dinner that same evening. They went straight from the dog sledge to the Christmas pots and pans, via the bathroom of course.

When the Christmas rush does finally start, two men fetch the decorations down from the loft and start to decorate the tree which, specially for the occasion, has been sent from heaven, meaning that it was dropped out of the Christmas flight over Daneborg ten days earlier. Someone else comes with a pile of records of Christmas music, takes off *The Electric Light Orchestra* from the record player and a moment later, Sirihus is echoing to the sounds of *A White Christmas* and similar songs.

The cooks, on such occasions, do not mind if others come into their kitchen; it is only Christmas once a year, and soon a delicious aroma of hot punch, pastries and traditional cakes is wafting around. There is definitely life and happiness in the kitchen.

While the radio operator is sweating away in his office to receive the many seasonal greetings to the patrol from far and near, the dining tables are set up in a large square and covered with decorated cloths and candles. Two hours after helping the last of the returning sledge teams, Sirihus is totally transformed. Christmas decorations hang everywhere and the smell of Christmas food, pine tree and vanilla mingle throughout the mess.

In general, our attitude to clothing is very relaxed; it is rare to see party clothes in Northeast Greenland where there is no real motive for dressing up. Christmas Eve, however, is an exception and tradition demands that people should be dressed in their finest. This they do, coming in one after the other from the cold outside, one man in particular looking a bit more uncomfortable than the rest because his collar and tie are too tight. Inside the mess, people stand for a while and shuffle awkwardly, uncomfortable in black polished shoes and fiddling with their collars, not really knowing what to do with their hands or what to say. It somehow doesn't seem appropriate to start a conversation about sledge dogs or the ideal length of a rope trace. After a glass of hot punch, however, reserve starts to melt away and discussions turn to sledge dogs and such things, even with a suit on.

Precisely because none of us has tired of Christmas music

throughout the previous weeks, or has had to fight his way through the city's neon-lit Christmas shopping madness, this evening is very special and happy. When the cooks call 'ready', it feels like a solemn ceremony and, with raised glasses, we toast the cooks and wish each other 'Happy Christmas'. Two hours later we can scarcely move, for seldom have so few eaten so much in such a short time.

After washing the dishes, we gather round the illuminated tree where greetings are read out, sent from different parts of the Defence Ministry and the Government with whom we have had radio contact. There are greetings, too, from earlier Sirius hands who have written to us with their thoughts and memories.

After a couple of hours of relaxed company and conversation, with plenty of candies to eat, people begin to take themselves quietly back to their rooms. Here they have more greetings and presents which were dropped from the plane, from families and friends in Denmark. Some close their doors behind them, wanting to be alone for a while at this moment, while others gather together in groups in their rooms to open presents and read their letters to each other.

Everyone is surprised to see how much the families at home have sent, though there are no bulky packets. This is thanks to the Sirius coordinator who will have notified the parents in good time of the maximum size of parcel that can be accepted, telling them that the packing will have to be very strong to withstand the air-drop.

The celebrations continue on Christmas Day but in a more relaxed way; the suits are put away with their mothballs again.

Although we have scarcely recovered after the Christmas Eve roast duck, another sledge team has taken over in the kitchen since early morning and the results of their efforts are laid out as a huge, luxurious lunch table. With this lunch and then the following day free, the Christmas holiday comes to an end, although the tree remains standing until New Year's Eve. This, of course, we also celebrate in the proper way, sitting around the table with silly paper hats on while the indoor fireworks are exploding on the table.

Outside, on the fjord, another bomb is set off exactly as the clock strikes midnight. This is very like the 'ship's bomb' of the summer time and for a brief moment, the whole of Daneborg is lit up by the explosion; Sirius Patrol greets the New Year.

January Days

Besides being the month for recovering strength before the long spring journey, January is in many ways a busy month. In Northeast Greenland, it is usually the month with the most frequent and violent snowstorms, the last snow-free patches become covered over and the snow surface takes on a more windswept appearance. In spite of the many storms, each of which can last a couple of days or more, January is also an optimistic time. At noon, when going for lunch, there is the heartening sight of steadily increasing light in the southern sky over Kap Breusing. Already by the middle of the month, the first reddening of the sky is visible. Once again, the sun begins to set fire to the heavens and it is easy to see how, in earlier days, folk worshipped the sun as a god and celebrated the solstices. Those who have experienced the winter's dark time know how much the sun means for man's mental state.

January is also the month when Sirius men try to get to grips with many different tasks. Both new and old Sirius hands now know their areas of responsibility and have to consider the future need for new materials and supplies. Everything that is in store is counted for an inventory and everyone is occupied daily with writing out order forms for new items that are going to be needed or for standard items that are in short supply. This will be the last chance to place such orders because of the time needed to get all the supplies together in Denmark. Everything that is ordered now, must be purchased and sent to Sirius' central packing station before being despatched to the docks for shipping. By the time we are back from our spring patrol journeys, it will be too late. Forget to order anything now and the earliest it will arrive is the following year.

Individual sledge teams will certainly have decided during the autumn journeys that there are some aspects of their own sledge equipment that they want to change or renew. Again, everyone has to consider how great their need is, or whether a particular piece of gear will last out another four or five months of sledging before being replaced.

Various bits of the station's equipment, such as the electrical generators and heaters, must also be serviced so that later, when there are only two men alone on the station, they will not be overwhelmed by technical problems.

Other projects for January include writing up all the wildlife sightings made by the sledge teams so that the data is recorded and ready for the scientists to consult. The first part of January also sees the writing of reports on the autumn journeys. As if this is not enough to fill the days, the normal life of the station must be attended to and the dogs kept in good training with, as a rule, a training run every second day.

Before anyone realises, January is almost over and one day the radio operator comes out of his shack and says: "The spring journey routes have arrived!"

6. Spring travel
THE LONG SLEDGE JOURNEY

Farewell and Welcome

Once again, the sledges are fully loaded outside Sirihus and ready to go.

Another departure hour is upon us. By now it is a familiar situation; excited barking from the dogs and disruption everywhere. The name of the month is about to change to February, but what lies ahead is the masterpiece, the spring patrol.

One of the objectives of this patrol is to show the flag along the whole length of the desolate coastal region of northeast Greenland so that there can no longer be any doubt as to which nation administers this huge territory. It stretches from Scoresbysund in the south, right round the north of Greenland to the Thule district in the north west.

So much for the fine words; not one of us gives them much thought as we offer each other a hand and say 'goodbye until the summer'. In this way, we take leave of our human friends but, in a few days time, we should be able to welcome the best friend of all, the sun.

It is not without some excitement that, on one of the first days in February at around noon, we can see a brief glow on the tops of the highest mountains, on the highest snows. It is fully three months since we last saw this sight and, because so much of our time has been spent out of doors, we are especially aware of the moment. It shows us just how grey and colourless everything has been through the middle of the winter, and we revel in the vision of these sun-tipped mountain tops. A few moments later and the glow has gone, but we know now that it will be back and that the days of the dark time are numbered.

The return of the sun means so much to us that we lie in the tent with the map spread out, trying to work out the best place from which to see the sun's disc for the first time. Prognoses of this kind are, of course, vague, and may well be delayed by poor travelling conditions or cloudy weather on the appointed day. Travelling far into the deep fjord systems can also delay the reunion for weeks because of the shadow of the high mountains round about.

At last, one beautiful day, the snow out ahead of us does become bright and sparkling. The dogs notice it too and increase their speed to reach it. To cheer them on, we call: "What is it dogs, can you see the sunlight?" We become quite nervous that we may not come out of the shadow in time; then, suddenly, our eyes are struck by the brilliant light and for one indescribable moment we can see the burning disc and, completely forgetting to narrow our eyes and squint, become momentarily blinded with dark spots dancing in front of our eyeballs. Stopping the dogs and grabbing the camera, we take at least half a dozen pictures of the sun, just like some tourist attraction that one has never seen before and may never see again.

Even though the sunlight is sharp and blinding there is no feeling of warmth on the skin but, in some almost-forgotten corner of the mind, a long-frozen lump begins to thaw!

11 + 2 = 13

Since old times, the number 13 has been surrounded by mystery and superstition. Even today, some people arrange invitations so that there will not be 13 sitting at the table and there are those who will be keeping a careful watch for black cats on the 13th day of the month. However, none of this has held Sirius back from choosing the number 13 as the ideal number for the total complement of a full sledge team: 11 dogs and two men!

Up until now, I have been describing the dogs anonymously and, in reality, it is not until the spring journey that the new hand really gets to know his dogs as individuals. To do them justice, each dog should have its own chapter in this book but I will at least introduce some of the members of sledge team two:

***Fumle*;** age 2½ years; weight 41 kg

In spite of his weight, Fumle is not the dominating type. He is good natured and quiet except when Piteraq, his neighbour, best friend and sworn enemy, irritates him too much. In fact, on one occasion, he got so mad with Piteraq that he shortened his nice bushy tail by about ten cm!

Either because he is a little unintelligent, or because he can be a bit withdrawn, Fumle can often be seen sitting, staring into the distance with a faraway philosophical look on his face. All the same, he is a good sledge dog who works willingly all day long, except for one instance when he suffered from constipation, giving rise to the following little episode:

It was really my fault because, for a while, we did not bother to unwrap the dog pemmican from its plastic packing. The plastic was quite thin and most dogs just tore it off and let it lie, but Fumle, unlike the other dogs who were just as hungry, ate the whole lot and his stomach could not cope with both. It was easy to see that he was unwell but, in spite of his strenuous efforts, nothing passed through and after a few days he was unable to keep up with the rest of the dogs. We decided to carry him on the sledge. This did not suit him at all and, to avoid it, he kept jumping off. In the end we had to tie him on top of the load to prevent him getting off.

A couple more days went by and still Fumle did not manage to pass anything, but sooner or later all things come to an end. One day, just as we had had a rest, something suddenly happened. Tavsur had walked ahead a short distance to reconnoitre our route, while I was standing with my back to the sledge studying the map, when I heard a characteristic noise. Oh no!

I turned round and there stood Fumle half upright on the sledge with a satisfied look on his face and it was all too obvious that he had got his bowels to work again.

"Well damn you, Fumle!" — he had been down on the ground to walk around barely two minutes beforehand. I jumped forward to get him off the sledge but he had already begun again to turn from side to side. I will not comment on what the uppermost sleeping bag came to look like before I managed to unclip him and drag him roughly overboard.

Tavsur in the meantime had heard my shout and come running back. We looked at each other, at the sleeping bag and then at each other again. It was Tavsur's sleeping bag on top! Tavsur yelled something not very flattering at Fumle who was by now standing a little distance away looking pleased with himself, whereafter Tavsur, with a resigned expression on his face, started to scrape the sleeping bag clean with his knife. While I stood and watched, I could not resist saying:

"Look on the bright side Tavsur, it seems as though Fumle will be alright now."

This remark did not seem to amuse him much so I said no more and I need hardly mention that Fumle did the rest of the day's travel on foot.

***Jessie*;** age nine months; weight 36 kg

Jessie is the team's new bitch, and is already a promising sledge dog. She is in many ways an unusual bitch pup and, almost from the first day, has kept her position in the team; she is calm and collected too; characteristics seldom found among the bitches. She also understands, in a remarkable way, how to share her favours equally between her two cavalier escorts, Duppen and Fyr, but there was one time when this caused a spell of trouble. It happened as follows:

It is always with a certain degree of pessimism that one awaits the time for a bitch to come in season. The calm and disciplined behaviour that have gradually become established in the team, disappear totally. The bitch becomes a lot more scheming than before, which as a rule is quite a lot, and her flirting with first one dog and then another, results in fight after fight between the rivals for her affections. Male dogs are male dogs and, for the weeks that the bitch is in season, there is an unusual lack of concentration on the work to be done. It is a time which can give the dogs grey hairs, as well as the Sirius men.

Now Jessie was, as already mentioned, an unusually good bitch who would as a rule stay in her place in the team, and Duppen and Fyr seemed to have a silent agreement to share her friendship and keep all the others away.

The Dog Man at Daneborg had given express instructions that Jessie, in due course, should be mated with a dog called Eigil. This was because Eigil was from the Thule district and represented a chance to introduce new blood into the team.

The whole team was in an uproar the evening that Eigil was put to Jessie to conclude the matter, and it was worst for Duppen and Fyr. Not understanding the real reasons, they blamed each other for the loss of Jessie to Eigil and for the first time they became serious deadly enemies. They were worthy opponents and they did not miss any opportunity to leap at each other, not giving Eigil another thought, although he was the unwitting cause of the whole upset and didn't even seem to care much about Jessie. Desperation took hold of them and from time to time they tried to mate with Jessie while we were travelling, even when we were going at a good speed, but as soon as one of them tried, the other would cross over to put a spanner in the works. This interfered with the driving more and more so that in the end the two traces for Duppen and Fyr had to be shortened, meaning that they could then no longer catch up with Jessie. This didn't solve the problem altogether for these two together were so strong that in good conditions they could pull the sledge almost by themselves. The whole situation was a mess, and each time these two managed to pull the sledge towards the target, Jessie, they invariably started to tear the fur out of each other. Because of the strife between two normally inseparable friends, the other dogs became disturbed as well and throughout that long week we had fight after fight. In addition to battles during the day, there was endless barking and howling to keep us awake all night, so it came as a huge relief when we discovered one day that Jessie was no longer in season. Immediately, Duppen and Fyr became the best of friends again and peace and discipline were restored to the whole team.

Moral ... no, I had better not say it!

Soth; age nine months; weight 35 kg

Soth is the street-wise boy of the team and in spite of his youth, is tough, self-confident and arrogant. He is a born fighter and lacks any respect for the older dogs, several of which have learnt to keep their distance from him. Arrogance and size are characteristics he has inherited from his father, Duppen,

Soth is one of the Sirius dogs born during a sledge journey, which also deserves a bit of explanation.

On my first spring journey, we had a snow-white bitch in the team called Jette, and when she came in season in the middle of February, it was Duppen who was chosen for her mate. Everything went as it should and some 65 days later, on 25 April 1978, Jette produced a black dog and a white bitch puppy. This happened at a place called Blå Sø (Blue Lake), lying in the inner part of Kronprins Christians Land near the appropriately named Nioghalvfjerdsfjord (Seventy Nine Fjord, the latitude on which it lies).

We knew the birth was imminent. Jette was looking tired all that day and had been let free from her trace to follow along behind at her own speed. In the evening she was given a place in the corner of the tent and next morning we witnessed the great moment when she gave birth to her puppies. Blind and helpless as they were, the travel had to continue, so I sewed up a travelling bag for the puppies out of two sheepskin kamiks, fastened a strap to the bag and carried it hanging against my stomach inside my shirt. This worked well and, for the next couple of weeks, I carried the puppies while we travelled. Jette was given her freedom for this time, riding on the sledge and every second hour having the puppies with her to feed them. While this was going on, we would have a cup of tea in peace and quiet.

Not all Sirius men are lucky enough to have puppies born on a journey, partly because the opportunity may not arise but also partly because they avoid it, thinking that it will slow them down and cause problems. In my opinion, this fear is unfounded and I think they miss out on a great experience.

Although it meant a little more load to pull and an inactive bitch riding on the sledge for a while, these were the only appreciable disadvantages for us and they were more than compensated for by the interest and amusement that a couple of puppies brought to our sledge journey.

Soth and his sister grew rapidly and became so chubby that, after 14 days, they no longer needed to be in their travel bag. In its place, we made a box for them, lined with the remains of an old sleeping bag and this became their home until we returned to Daneborg seven weeks later.

It was fascinating to see how quickly they began to develop into small sledge dogs. At only one month old, they could sit up on their fat backsides and in their squeaky treble voices start to howl at the sky. Of course, they were only trying to imitate the adult dogs but the first time that they succeeded, they seemed quite surprised.

In the first weeks, Jette and the puppies had their space in the corner of the tent but, by the middle of May, it was becoming so warm that they preferred to be outside. The puppies could still run freely around the camp and at one month old, they began to indulge in the usual puppyish activities such as playing with anything that was loose. As a rule, they slept while we drove along and were therefore fresh and ready to play their games when we wanted to get some sleep.

Of course, they could not work out where we went when we crawled into our sleeping bags, so they had to investigate this more thoroughly. For us, this meant being awoken from deep sleep by something running over the sleeping bag. On drowsily opening our eyes, there would be two small and very curious puppies standing on top of us and staring intently at us with their small wrinkled eyes. Each time they did this, they were so startled by our waking up that they would rush out of the tent, upsetting all the pots and pans and anything else that stood in their way.

Whatever else these two small bandits had in common, it seemed that they both had a poor memory. Ten minutes later, just as we had fallen asleep again, they found it essential to see if we were still in the sleeping bags. In spite of all this, the puppies were firm favourites and for the first ten or15 times we managed to laugh at such antics. Finally it became too much for our sense of humour and when the puppies had hurtled out of the tent yet again at their usual speed, the tunnel door of the tent was firmly closed behind them! Many happy times were spent watching those two energy bombs as they grew up and later I chose the black male, Soth, for my team while the bitch went to another team.

Fyr: age three years; weight: 39 kg

Fyr is the team's bright guy. He is also the best lead dog and is used in front when the snow becomes so deep and loose that, instead of running the dogs in a fan, we hitch them up in a 'Nome' system (two by two in pairs behind Fyr) or in 'Tandem' (singly, one behind the other in a long line).

Only a few dogs have the right qualities to become a leader. It requires self-confidence, intelligence and the acceptance of the other dogs. Fyr has all these characteristics but does not seem to want to lead and becomes bored when he is not side by side in company with Duppen.

Apart from this, Fyr is a splendid dog at all times and is the extrovert of the whole team. He has a permanently good temper that I have only ever seen him lose once, during the brief spat with Duppen. His enthusiasm for life and his good nature are so astonishing that, on days when one's own mood is a little sad, he is a great boost to morale. On top of all this, he has developed into the best sledge puller ever, and if the reader could but see what I have seen Fyr do, he would have to agree that there isn't an animal on earth that can compare with the Greenland dog when it comes to sheer muscle power and a willingness to give one hundred *per cent.* 20,000 km is said to be a normal distance for a Sirius dog to travel in its working life, a distance roughly equal to half the earth's circumference. Fyr deserves, as do all the other Sirius dogs, the greatest respect; without dogs like this, there would not be anything called the Sirius Sledge Patrol.

Flying High...

It has been the practice for many years that some sledge teams are carried by plane to North Greenland, in order to be able to patrol as much as possible of the northern parts of the area over which Sirius has the obligation to maintain Danish sovereignty. Since Sirius does not have its own plane, assistance is given by the Air Force who take responsibility for the transport of dogs, men and equipment to North Greenland every spring, (plate 7).

Unfortunately, there are not many places up there where a large Hercules aircraft can land and Station Nord is most often used, even though it is not ideal in many ways and is a notorious snow hole with very high snow fall. Sirius takes advantage of whatever is available. A smaller, short take-off and landing plane, flying to different locations, would be far preferable, but it is a question of available money and this has to be decided by other authorities. (In fact, smaller Twin Otter aircraft are being used nowadays).

We were one of three teams flown, on 1 March 1978, to Station Nord from where we would continue sledging in our different directions. The homeward journey to Daneborg would be made on our own feet, but that problem was still two months ahead. First we had to patrol North Greenland and, at the beginning of March up there, I experienced the coldest and most unpleasant days of my whole time with Sirius.

A couple of days after starting our journey, my partner and I were on our way up onto a stretch of the inland ice in Kronprins Christians Land. Our target was Romer Sø where there was a sledging depot. One afternoon while we were travelling on the inland ice, the temperature quite suddenly started to plummet. It was calm, clear weather which, at that time of year, is usually a sign that conditions will become seriously cold. A fog of frozen breath rose from the dogs and ourselves, forming a vapour trail which hung silently in the air behind us. Real cold, in my opinion, means a temperature below minus 40°C. Up to this point it is not too unpleasant in the dry arctic air, as long as there is no wind. I have often noticed that, for me, the cold starts to become uncomfortable at exactly minus 43°C.

When it is this cold, the snow seems to change structure, its friction against the sledge runners increases, and one can almost hear how differently the sledge moves over the snow.

On this particular day, we were in no doubt that it was bitterly cold and we could follow, on our thermometer, just how amazingly fast the temperature fell. Within one hour it had dropped from minus 38°C to minus 50°C and at that stage the dogs themselves began to suffer, initially with sore feet. They walked awkwardly as if they were stepping on burning coals and, because of this and the poor sliding quality of the snow, we made very slow progress. After four and a half hours, when we saw the thermometer standing at minus 55°C, we decided to stop and camp.

To put up the tent in such cold is not at all pleasant since some parts of the job just cannot be done with mittens on. Each time we touched a piece of metal, it was like a burn; fingers would stick to the metal and become stiff and unmoveable in a very short time. There was nothing for it but to light the primus outside and set it in the half-erected tent so that the indoors man could warm, and invariably burn, his cold fingers. Once the tent was finally up, the outdoors man had to get inside and warm himself before he could finish his outside jobs; something that was unheard of under normal conditions.

Finally camp was set up, but we then discovered that we had made a miscalculation over the distance to the Romers Sø depot, I don't recall exactly how much, but at least one day's travel. Furthermore we had not been making as good progress as we expected, so that even though we had brought some reserve provisions, it turned out that they would only last for one more camp and we were still 60 km from the depot. Even under normal conditions, this would have been a cause of some worry because of the unpredictable weather. If the temperature stayed at its present very low level, we had the added prospect of slow sledging to the depot and must therefore start to ration our remaining supplies. The consequence of this was that we had to turn off the primuses shortly after we had made our meal, just when we had the most need for warmth. Even with a good sleeping bag, it can be difficult to stay warm throughout the night at such low temperatures. I woke at three in the morning with my teeth chattering.

It is no joke to make four or five hours pass in a sleeping bag, wide awake and frozen, unless you are a complete masochist! If, at the same time, peaceful snoring is coming from the other side of the tent, the inescapable thought is: "What the hell am I doing here while all normal people are at home in Denmark eating their breakfast?" I shall stop this sermon on self pity, or rather save it for later, because of course, the choice had been mine.

At last, the clock showed that it was time to light up the primuses for breakfast. What a treat to feel a little warmth, but a quick look outside soon dispelled the feeling of good humour; the temperature outside was no longer minus 55°C, it was minus 57°C, and we had no choice but to continue.

As I wrote in my diary, it was a tough day, especially for the dogs, and we had a major problem to stay warm.

Managing to make only four km per hour, we drove 20 km in the temperature of minus 57°C and the day ended abruptly when we reached the vertical glacier-edge and looked down onto the frozen surface of Romer Sø. How far down it was, I am not sure, perhaps 20 to 30 metres, but certainly too far to jump. There were also crevasses along the edge, into which the snow would disappear with a swoosh and this did nothing to increase our happiness. There was no way down at this point and we would have to retrace our steps and find another way off the glacier. It was already too dark to look that day.

The situation was by now reasonably predictable so we thought we would trust to luck and use up the last of the dog food. We also decided to share out our own food between us, apart from a little oatmeal for the next morning. Again, we had to turn off the heat and again, I awoke five hours earlier than planned and yes, but I have said all that!

The next morning it was quite clear that if we were not going to go to bed hungry that night, we had to reach the depot during the coming day. As soon as it was light enough, we put on skis and set about finding a place to get off the glacier, leaving the dogs behind and, because of the crevasse danger, we were roped together for safety.

At last we had some luck and found a steep but feasible snow ramp where it might be possible to drive the sledge down onto the lake. We hurried back to camp a few km away, collected the dogs and gear and were delighted to find that the temperature had risen ... to minus 47°C!

Soon we were back at the snow fan and the descent went well. Putting chains around the runners to act as brakes, we hung on to the sledge as long as we could until, near the bottom, we let it go by itself and tobogganed the rest of the way. Now we had only 40 km left to run, but the dogs had lost their enthusiasm in the low temperatures and we had to ski ahead of them the whole way to get them to pull.

After nine hours of slogging, we finally reached the depot and thought our sufferings were at an end which, of course, experience should have told us they were not. The next couple of days were roughly as follows:

The depot hut was unusually small, less than ten square metres and, in spite of repeated attempts, it was impossible to light the paraffin stove. We had been really looking forward to some warmth at last, but the only result of dismantling the stove and trying to repair it was that we got very dirty. Finally we had to give up and light our own primuses and set them down in the very small space available.

Not long after, first one primus and then the other started to splutter and go out so that, in no time at all, the hut was filled with extremely unpleasant paraffin fumes. It turned out that the paraffin was old and full of impurities. We tried to filter out the dirt and then re-start the primuses, but our eyes began to itch and burn, caused by one or other of the impurities in the paraffin, and we got 'fueleye' which feels a bit like having sand in one's eyeballs.

For the sake of the dogs, we had intended to take two days rest at this god-forsaken place. There was plenty to do since almost half of the dogs had developed open sores on their feet in the intense cold. This meant that we had to sew about 20 dog boots from our old socks and any old clothing we could spare. We could hardly focus on the sewing with our inflamed and running eyes and, from my diary, I read that I had sores on my fingers and blisters on my feet as well as two patches of frostbite on my face. Well, the next day we would, with luck, be moving on and the next stage promised to be a tough undertaking. We had 15 days sledging to the next depot, if all went well, and this time we would make sure we had sufficient supplies. 15 days plus 50%, say 22 days of supplies plus a cold weather reserve. We soon sorted out all that was necessary and I anticipated that the sledge loads would be around 550 to 650 kg, which is heavy enough! Never mind, just as long as we got out of this damned fix, everything would be OK.

It was not to be. The next day there was a heavy storm blowing outside the hut and a temperature of minus 34°C. Any thought of continuing the journey was out of the question; it was simply no weather to send a dog out!

What can one do on such a day of bad weather lie-up? Lean back in a chair and devote oneself to flights of the imagination through the world's great literature?

Yes, it can sometimes be like that, but with inflamed eyes that would scarcely open for the pain, reading was not an attractive option and in the lower bunk, which was on the floor, life was further complicated by the need to wear mittens. The hut was so draughty that if one put a cup of hot coffee on the floor, it would be frozen solid in a couple of hours.

For two more days, this awful weather persisted. It was too cold to sit up, so there was nothing for it but to lie in the sleeping bags, feel miserable and be philosophical about it. My god, there was a lot of philosophy!

We made sporadic attempts to read and I see from my diary that I was trying to get acquainted with a book by Anders

Bodelsen called ... *Freezing Point*!

In this situation, there is always one question to be answered, for the benefit of the uninitiated, and that is how does one go to the toilet in a raging snow storm or in a temperature of minus 57°C? Let me elaborate. No, it does not freeze so quickly that one must carry an axe, but one soon learns to do what has to be done without any unnecessary dawdling and to go only when it can no longer be held in!

Everything comes to an end sometime and on the fifth day, fine weather returned; calm, silent and minus 40°C. How lovely it was to close the door behind us and leave this crappy little hut, which I heartily hope has long since been blown away. The only reason we had not used the tent was that it needed to be dried out ready for the next 15 days of journeying.

We got the sledge loaded and began to harness the dogs. Half of them needed kamiks on their sore feet but very few of them appreciated this sensitivity to their problems and, as soon as our backs were turned, they were busy trying to bite them off again; there could well have been some hard words said that morning. Yes, minus 40°C, lacing up home-made boots on the feet of obstinate dogs; anyone could be forgiven for using words not to be found in an ordinary dictionary. Neither of us had any worry about yelling at the dogs for there has always been a saying amongst polar travellers that when, one day, we come to stand in front of Saint Peter and confess our sins, forgiveness will always be granted to those who have in past times been driven to terrible cursing by the obstinacy of sledge dogs!

At long last we could shout: "Yes, let's go dogs!" and as a final insult, half a dozen dog boots went flying past our ears! All that care not to overtighten them, and this was the only thanks we got. It must have taken us at least an hour to get away from that place.

To finish the story, we reached the next depot after only 14 days of sledging and our bad eyes healed within a couple of days, but it was a long time before the dogs' feet were once again healed and back to normal. We had to carry one dog on the sledge for more than a week, its ankle damaged by a kamik that was laced up too tightly. Psychologically too, the dogs were badly affected and for weeks we had to change our routine so that one of us skied out in front of them until they regained their interest in pulling forwards. I shall not forget it in a hurry that time when we were flown to Romer Sø in the far north, and the temperature plummeted.

Bear!

"Woof, woof," the sound comes softly from outside the tent.

In my sleepy state it seems far away but, after it is repeated a couple of times, alarm bells begin to ring loudly in my head. I am wide awake in a moment and listening anxiously.

"Woof," comes again from one of the dogs.

"Bear!" we say to each other at the same moment. Tavsur also has woken up at the sounds which are the dogs' unique way of alerting us to the fact that there is something unknown or dangerous out there in the dark, almost always a polar bear.

In violent haste we get out of our bags; Tavsur is quickest this time, and by the light of a match, I find our flare pistol and throw it out to him. After a hasty look, he crawls right out and dispels the darkness by firing a flare. After a moment, it lights up the whole area around our camp and the snow-covered fjord, with a bright white light. First he has a quick look at the dogs who are all sitting and staring in the same direction. Following their line of sight, he just catches a glimpse of a shadow disappearing into the darkness, before the flare burns out. I have come outside too and for safety, we fire an extra flare but it reveals nothing this time.

Well, we will probably not see anything more tonight; two flares are enough to scare off most bears. We hurry back to our sleeping bags. It is cold outside, but when there is a bear in the vicinity, one doesn't waste time putting on outer clothing. It is a matter of getting out of the tent and scaring the beast away before it does any damage.

With no more worries, we lie down to sleep again, safe in the knowledge that the dogs will warn us if the bear comes back; yet another situation where the dogs are invaluable to us.

It is remarkable how sensitive one becomes after a while, to the sounds of the dogs. One can sleep easily and remain undisturbed if they howl a bit or bark at each other a little, but yet learn to wake from even the deepest sleep when the dogs give their quiet warning 'woof'!

One of us will also have to get out of the sleeping bag if their barking becomes more excited. This usually means that they have pulled up the anchor at the end of the chain they are fastened to. If we do not move as fast as lightning on such an occasion, the orderly line of dogs can, in an instant, become a furry mass of maddened and desperate animals, biting and snarling in all directions.

Coming out too late to prevent such a fight, there is only one reasonable and humane way to stop it and that is to take the *Red Worm* and jump, yelling like a fiend, into the mass of dogs while kicking and lashing out on all sides.

It may sound brutal and it is, but these are not ordinary lap dogs that we are dealing with. Such treatment has a surprising ability to stop the panic and fear which are often the real cause of the dogs starting to fight; they see that they are getting tangled up in the loose chain and become frightened. One thing is certain; it is very stupid to use hands in such a tangle before the last dog has been silenced. Once all the dogs have learnt, through this heavy handed treatment, that someone is in charge, they take notice and calm down. They can then be handled without danger and the tangles can be sorted out. I have never yet seen a man get bitten undeservedly by a Sirius dog!

We were correct and there was no more bear trouble that night but the following morning we found the footprints about 150 metres from the tent. To judge from the size of the tracks, it was one of two half-grown animals we had passed the previous day and which must have followed our sledge tracks.

That day after the bear visit was to turn out to be proof of the fact that life on a long sledge journey is seldom boring. It became the longest day of our spring journey, 78 km as the crow flies, although in reality five to ten km more of actual travelling, as I will relate:

We had no advance expectations of such a big day. Where we had put up our tent, beneath Payers Tinde (Payers Peak) in Kejser Franz Joseph Fjord, there was half a metre of deep, loose snow which had been hindering us and making it hard going throughout the preceding days. In order to get clear of this soup-like surface we did not head directly towards our target, Antarctic Sund, but made a small detour to the mouth of Isfjord where we were almost sure there would be bare ice. Quite correct, and after a couple of hours of driving, with the dogs almost swimming in the deep snow, we finally reached the mouth of the fjord. Yes, there was bare ice out there but also quite a wind, to judge by the shimmering air. The weather was a bit depressing with a grey sky which threatened snow to come so, while we still had some shelter, we decided to take a tea break.

As usual, we talked a bit to the dogs and tidied up the tangled traces, it being the younger dogs as usual that had not been keeping to their proper places in the fan. But we had to get on with the day and soon we were out on the ice where we came upon some old sledge tracks, left from a time when there had been snow cover on the now bare fjord ice. What was left were the tracks from the sledge runners, looking like a railway track, with 44 miniature snow pyramids left by the dogs' feet.

Our team was, as always, very interested to meet old tracks and started to follow them, sniffing closely, but they were going in the wrong direction for us, back into Isfjord. Tavsur ran ahead for a while to lead the dogs back onto the correct course, a method we used from time to time instead of verbal commands, when there was a big change of direction to make. Rounding the headland into the fjord, a piercing wind came to meet us and I was so busy pulling on my windproof gear that I did not have a sufficiently good hold of the sledge; quite unexpectedly, it started to run away ahead of me and at the same moment, Tavsur shouted: "Bear!"

Warned by the shout, I could see the two polar bears, one large female with a small one-year-old cub, coming directly towards us from Isfjord and not yet aware of us, thanks to the wind direction. I just managed to grab hold of the sledge and throw myself onto it; lucky, because the dogs swung in towards the bears and Tavsur was already left behind. At a crazy speed we raced towards the bears, perhaps only 250 metres away. Damn! Now they have seen us and are standing still as if stunned.

I yelled and screamed at the dogs to try to stop them, and tried to turn the sledge over onto its side, but all in vain. I couldn't get much grip on the smooth ice and was in danger of losing my grip on the sledge. Would the mother bear stand or flee? The adrenaline began to pump through my veins. The mother bear tried to get our scent but then turned and followed her cub, which was already on the run.

Phew! I could breathe more easily and I managed to scramble on top of the sledge. I must put the break chains on. Hanging over the front of the sledge, not so easy with skis on, I got the chains over the points of the runners ... but they didn't have that much effect on the hard icy surface.

The bear cub could not keep up the speed and we were gaining on them. I yelled at the dogs again but they didn't care; they smelled blood. I tried to get the rifle, but the zipper on the rifle bag was being awkward and the wind was ice-cold and penetrating. I almost lost a mitten but managed to prepare the rifle and look up. The female bear had stopped and reared up on her back feet, facing us. Disaster seemed unavoidable, but suddenly, the dogs turned away. It was the cub they were interested in and we passed the mother only a few metres away. I calmed down a bit when I realised what was happening, but let off a volley of swearing at my disobedient mob. Gradually they ran out of steam and turned out into the fjord, away from both bears. Wiping the sweat from my forehead, I looked back but the bears were already far behind and disappearing behind a projecting ice block. I was really mad with the dogs. Stopping them at last, I jumped up off the sledge and grabbed *Red Worm* ... but wait: I was even madder with myself because I was unable to control them. That is what really counted and it was a bitter pill to swallow.

Still fuming, I took off the brake chains and headed back towards Tavsur, slowly regaining my temper and feeling relieved that nothing nasty had happened; a direct confrontation with the female bear was avoided as much by luck as by skill. Tavsur was glad to see us again, having felt a bit left out of it when the bear, the dogs and I disappeared from view.

Soon we were back on course and neither of us had time to think about what could have happened if we had taken another couple of minutes for our tea break; a sledge journey is full of such if's and maybe's. If one worried about them all, one would become a nervous wreck or not dare to do anything. Things went very well after that and, a couple of hours later, we reached Antarctic Sund. We took off our skis and changed to riding on the sledge; a little cold, but we were hindering rather than helping by trying to ski on the shiny ice. We had some fun as we drove on by throwing small pieces of paper at the dogs. The following wind which blew a little faster than we were travelling, carried the bits of paper forward and the dogs, already excited by the bear episode, went crazy chasing after them. When a piece of paper suddenly stopped and stuck in an uneven patch of ice, the dogs were nearly run down by the sledge careering up behind them on the slippery surface.

In this way we drove into Antarctic Sund in high good humour. As we reached the south end where we should really have camped, we found all the snow gone and the wind was becoming so strong that it was beginning to cause us problems. In a relatively few minutes, the situation changed from being near perfect to a little critical. Besides the increasing wind, the ice was changing character; up until now it had been very slightly rough on the surface, but it now became so smooth that the dogs themselves could hardly get any grip at all and the sledge began to pull them rather than the other way round. We jumped off the sledge and tried as best we could to control its violent weaving from side to side, while skating along with one of us on each side. Things would not have been so bad if the ice had been a clean unbroken surface, but there were a number of old leads (cracks) about 20 centimetres deep and almost as wide; it didn't require much imagination to realise the consequences of hitting one of these sideways at a speed of something like 20 km per hour.

Minute by minute, the wind increased in strength, while the dogs showed signs of becoming scared and a little desperate as they were increasingly buffeted by the gale and becoming tangled in their traces. Some of them gave up and lay down, letting themselves be dragged along behind the sledge. This couldn't continue for long. Time after time we only just managed to heave the sledge around before going sideways into a crack and with difficulty, we managed to bring the whole circus to a stop before someone got hurt or something got broken.

The only sensible solution seemed to be to drive against the wind and head towards the shore; it was fast becoming dangerous where we were. More crawling than upright, one of us went ahead of the dogs while the other pushed the sledge ahead in small jerks, most of the dogs having their work cut out just to stay upright. It took time, but at last we reached land near Skildvagten (the Sentinel), as the mountain at that point is called. Here the wind was nowhere near as strong and, close to the land, there was even a thin layer of snow on top of the ice, giving us enough grip to carry on in a more normal fashion; within ten minutes we found ourselves in complete calm. Taking a much-needed break, we stood and listened to the deep roaring of the wind out on the sound. The storm was increasing in strength again. We looked at each other with the unspoken thought; we were glad not to be out there.

Having come so far, we agreed to carry on for another 25 km to Ella Ø. The sky had cleared up and changed character during the course of the day but it still did not look that promising, with newly formed storm clouds visible. This could be a warning signal that a real east coast storm was on the way and, if we had to be anywhere in such a storm, there was nowhere we would rather be than the Ella Ø station.

On our way over Kempe Fjord in the darkness, we became more and more convinced that there was a major blizzard coming. The air was clear and shimmery and the twilit sky took on a dangerous character while threatening-looking lenticular black clouds formed overhead. The temperature confirmed our fears, having gone up from minus 22°C to minus 10°C. In the last ten km to Ella Ø it began to snow into our faces. Both we and the dogs were tired when at last we reached shelter. It was eight o'clock in the evening. and, to say the least, it had been an eventful ten-hour day. Now it could blow as much as it liked; we were, in any case, planning a rest day here in this beautiful place.

There is more about Ella Ø later in the book but suffice it to say that, about one hour after our arrival, we were sitting cosily inside the door of Pynten, as one of the huts at the station is called, and eating as much fried egg and bacon as we could manage. The eggs had been left by Sirius people who were living here the previous summer. Already, when they left Ella Ø, the hard frosts had begun and so the eggs had kept fresh. The only difference from normal fresh eggs was the yolk which, after a spell in the deep freeze, does not spread out; it stays in a small golden ball in the middle of the egg-white.

That evening was pure pleasure. The storm roared outside our cosy quarters, the coffee kettle was simmering on the stove with freshly brewed coffee, while the air was full of the smell of newly-baked white bread.

By tradition when we had a day off, we unpacked our cassette player with its five accompanying tapes and thawed them out; there were music and happy times in Pynten that evening and we had a long talk about our favourite subjects: Sirius, Northeast Greenland, wildlife, music and a whole lot more. It was a happy situation; no thought for tomorrow and free from the worries and misery of the rest of the world; things which we could do nothing about anyway!

The storm calmed down the day after our arrival but turned instead into a heavy snowfall which delayed our departure for two more days. We had everything we needed where we were and the delay was a good opportunity to repair some of the damage done by a 'bear visit' which of course the station had suffered since the previous summer. We use the expression 'bear visit' whenever a bear has broken into a depot or hut. By chance, it was here at Ella Ø that I saw my first bear.

That happened on my first spring journey when, one February day, we arrived at the station.

"Damn, there is a bear in there," said my partner.

It was a little while before I saw it because I was looking for something white, whereas polar bears are more yellowish when compared to the whiteness of snow. Anyway, there it was and at a distance of half a kilometre, I could see two animals walking around between the huts. It didn't take long before they spotted us and quickly disappeared behind a nearby hill.

I was quite sad not to get a chance to take a couple of photos, but my partner reassured me that I would have plenty more chances some other time. That was a small consolation.

We reached the station and stopped the dogs. Hell, what a mess. Everywhere there were cans of food lying about the place that looked as though they had been used as targets for rifle shooting, peppered with holes made by the bear's teeth.

We left the dogs to stand and guard the sledge while we looked around to assess the damage. When we came to the provisions hut we could hardly believe our eyes. A bear had torn off one wall of the hut in much the same way as we would tear open a packet of oatmeal. Outside the hut there were thousands of kroners worth of food while inside, not only were the shelves empty, they were smashed into firewood. Food covered the floor to a depth of 20 to 30 cm, mostly split open and mixed thoroughly with bear droppings.

"There goes our day off at Ella Ø," said my partner stating the obvious, since naturally we could not leave the station in such a mess. Everything would have to be cleaned up and repaired and an inventory made of what food was still useable. It would take at least two days, which was all we could spare if we were to keep to our schedule. Bad luck!

First of all we had to get the dogs properly spanned and fed since, against our normal practice, we had just left them lying where we had stopped.

"Woof," came suddenly from Lyn (Lightning).

He sat and stared fixedly at the hut where the dog food was stored, which we had not yet visited.

"Bear," shouted my partner and, sure enough, out of a broken window in the dog food hut less than 50 metres from us, a bear appeared. For several moments, it stood and blinked sleepily at us before quietly wandering off in the footsteps of its comrades.

Lucky; I was glad we had not already gone in to get food for our dogs. I didn't like the thought that I might have walked straight into that dark hut, and come face to face with a sleeping bear, maybe thinking it was just a bag of dried fish, but it would have made a good story!

"Whatever next," said my partner: "There are bears every damn where," but we still had to get food for our dogs.

We knocked politely on the front door of the hut to give any other sleeping guests the chance to leave peacefully. There were no more, but it was clear that there had been a party in there. Sacks of dried fish and boxes of dog pemmican were scattered around in total confusion, and the copious amounts of bear droppings suggested that the guests had not been hungry when they left the feast. We sighed.

Next day, the big job of clearing up began and we found that the bears had not been completely stupid; they had paid special attention to certain delicacies. Dried milk powder seemed to have struck them as particularly excellent and we filled two large rubbish sacks with empty dried milk containers, finding only two tins that had escaped attention. On the other hand, they had given the tinned dinners a wide berth, but that was understandable! I hardly remember how many sacks we filled with spoiled provisions but I guess it was ten or 20.

Inside the hut we started to shovel from each end and worked towards each other, sorting the food as we went. Quite suddenly we began to feel a strong urge to sneeze; we had reached the place where a large box of black pepper lay smashed and mixed up with kilos of oatmeal. From the depths of my heart, I hoped that the bears had got a noseful when they had broken open that pepper box.

While we were occupied with filling rubbish sacks and moving them down onto the ice for burning, we noticed a yellow blob approaching from out on the fjord. Yes, it was a bear which, in spite of our presence and the barking of the dogs, seemed to be bold enough to walk straight up to the dog food store as if walking home. It stopped in surprise and then looked accusingly at us because we had put shutters over the broken window.

This time we could take photographs of the beast and I filmed him as he reared up on his hind legs and smashed the shutters so that wood splinters went flying everywhere. He used his powerful claws like a crowbar, but when the whole window began to give way under the attack, we fired a couple of light flares at him to scare him away. We had had enough of bears sleeping in the dog food hut.

Later in the day, a second sledge team arrived and one of the two Sirius men was, most conveniently, a skilled carpenter; just what we needed, as the whole wall of the food store had to be repaired.

After two days, the station was beginning to look more or less back to normal, but it was only a brief respite. It turned out that by summertime, when the station was permanently manned again, the bears had once more attacked the provisions hut. This time they had overturned the other half of the wall. It was the last straw. The following summer the hut was strengthened with heavy wooden sheathing and has stood up to bear attacks ever since.

Of course, it was not just on Ella Ø that bears made life difficult for sledge teams and in the southern part of the patrol's area, there are a number of small cabins from the old trapper's era which from time to time the patrol uses for over-night stays. For the most part, these are only four to six square metres in size and built out of three-quarter-inch wooden boarding covered with felt. They are easy targets for the bears and it sometimes seems as though certain bears have made a speciality of going from hut to hut, eating what provisions and dog food they can find and then having fun by knocking holes in the walls just to annoy the Sirius men. One could be forgiven for thinking that these small huts were, in general, poorly made and ready to fall over at the least provocation, but not so; I have never heard of a trapper's hut being damaged by even the worst storms, but a hungry bear passing by is another story altogether. Once he has got into the hut, either by tearing away the door or a window, and has eaten what he can, he will seldom walk out by the same way, to the great annoyance of the Sirius men. Perhaps it is due to a sudden attack of claustrophobia, but whatever the reason, as well as the smashed window or torn off door, there is nearly always a large gaping hole in the opposite wall where the bear has apparently just jumped out through the wood. This is clear evidence of the enormous power and weight of these animals; the wood normally is not just broken but completely smashed to splinters as if it has undergone an attack by an axe maniac!

When one finds such a hut where the bear has, in what seems like fun, taken the coal stove outside and dropped it in the snow, it begins to look like pure vandalism. The smashed huts did not mean any real danger for us on sledge journeys because we always had our tent and only used the huts for comfort and a change. The loss of dog food and provisions were, however, potentially serious because we always counted on being able to stock up with new supplies at huts and it could be a real problem finding a raided depot, when the last food on the sledge had just been used up.

The ravaging of our depots by bears in the years 1977-79 was not exactly a new phenomenon, but it certainly appeared to be on the increase. Since the Northeast Greenland National Park was set up in 1974, all wildlife, including polar bears, have been given total protection throughout the area. Not that I am in any way critical of this change because I, for one, have always thought that a polar bear skin looked best on a living bear!

Whether or not the polar bear population has increased due to its protection, is so far uncertain, but it has to be remembered that before protection came into force, the total kill of bears within the area of the park was only between five and ten per year. That the attacks on huts and depots is increasing year by year, may be due more to the possibility that the bears which would hitherto have been shot are the ones that have become 'hut bears'. This is born out by our observation that the bears we saw around the huts and depots were much more aggressive and careless than the so-called 'wild' bears which we used to meet along the outer coast. These latter usually fled as soon as they got wind of us and they probably live all their lives out in the pack ice, hunting for their traditional food, seals; never acquiring a taste for tins and packets.

Since the start of protection, these 'hut bears' seem to have developed their techniques substantially and I believe some of them have learnt simply to follow our tracks from depot to depot. As an instance of the bear problem, in the spring of 1979, more than half of the depots that Tavsur and I used had been damaged to some extent.

One could, with good reason, ask the Sirius people why they do nothing to protect their depots. They do, so far as is possible! For example, new bear-proof depot huts are being built when the money is available. To make them bear-proof, the outside is made quite smooth by using plywood sheets and flush fitting doors and windows so that there is nowhere for the bear's strong claws to get any purchase. These new huts are made from prefabricated sections, insulated and so solid that even a polar bear will give up trying to make a hole in the wall.

It takes a lot of time and money to build new huts like this over the whole of the patrol area, so in the days which I am writing about, we used some other tricks to make life more difficult for hungry hut bears. All the dog food was enclosed in steel wire containers made from finger-thick steel wire. The enormous strength of the bears can be judged from the fact that they still managed to carry, apparently without difficulty, one of these containers weighing 200 to 300 kg and drop it some distance away from the depot. As a rule they failed to get at the contents, but this was scant comfort to us when the container was found half-buried in the solid fjord-ice, needing to be dug out and carried back to the depot. Bear-safe, yes, but fairly safe from us too because in this instance, the container was frozen lid downwards into the snow so that it could not be opened. Perhaps we should have anchored the containers down as well, but everything takes time and whenever something new is tried it is a year at least before the results can be evaluated. We had no prejudice against inventions and new ideas, but the time pressure was often such that in the short while at our disposal, it was difficult to turn theory into practice.

When it came to man-food supplies, we enclosed these in heavy steel boxes with strong locks; that should have been enough! Again, the problem was that if the bear could not open the boxes, it often dragged them a long way, usually out onto the fjord.

Sometimes the bear managed to open the cases by strength or cunning. One type of box, it was soon discovered, could be squeezed open, probably by jumping up and down on top of it. Another type of steel box showed that bears, besides their colossal strength, could show considerable intelligence and ingenuity. The box could not be opened by brute force, but the bears found that it could be opened by somehow loosening the locking system.

It is common enough to hear 'bear stories' which are almost unbelievable and greatly overdramatised; I quite understand that anyone who has never experienced the capabilities of a polar bear is liable to be sceptical of these tales, since I myself could sometimes scarcely believe my own eyes when I saw the results of the bears' strength and cunning. There have been situations where I have thought to myself: 'that is just not possible!'

Anyone could be forgiven for asking whether a Sirius man might not become very tired of polar bears?

For myself, I can answer, "Yes, but mostly no."

Yes, because of course, one curses the bears to hell whenever it is discovered that they have taken or ruined all the provisions and the dog food. It is also no fun to have to shovel 15 cubic metres of snow out of a hut where a bear has forgotten to shut the door behind him!

But no! No, because the polar bear is the living symbol of the country itself, of Northeast Greenland, untamed, majestic and powerful.

It is a magnificent sight to see a polar bear in these surroundings where only nature itself determines the limits to its movements. That they can be difficult, sometimes dangerous and often irritating, makes them somehow more valued by those of us who experience them in their real environment.

I hope, too, that while there is still time, all of us will understand the need for their protection and come to respect both the bears and all the other creatures who share this planet with us and who enjoy life and freedom as much as we do ourselves.

A sense of springtime in March

Spring is, in my opinion, the most beautiful of the seasons, whether in Northeast Greenland or any other part of the world.

We are not yet used to the warmth and the sunshine and thus we value all the more every moment of these life-giving elements.

In Northeast Greenland, it feels as though the sun and the cold are eternally fighting a hard and pitiless battle. In February, the sun makes brief, but increasingly lengthy appearances over the horizon each day, as if to assess its still overwhelmingly powerful opponent. In March the sun begins its attack in earnest but the cold still responds violently and the sun is, as a rule, reduced merely to lighting the landscape; it does not yet have enough power to give any warmth. At the same time, March can bring some big surprises in this respect. Our experiences that took place during the big freeze at Romer Sø on my first spring journey, occurred around 10 March. Exactly one year after this, Tavsur and I find ourselves travelling much further south through Alpefjord which is, in my opinion, the most beautiful fjord in the whole of Northeast Greenland.

As we enter Alpefjord, it looks very much like all the others.

The mountains that surround it have been eroded through time in a way that is typical of the mountains in Northeast Greenland. Half way in to the fjord, however, a view opens up that has no equal. Steep mountains with sharp pointed summits spread out in front of our wondering eyes. These are the Staunings Alps.

Still further into the fjord, the vista becomes even more majestic and a world unfolds that dwarfs any man-made architecture. Greatest of all is the innermost part of Alpefjord, which has the name Dammen (the Pond).

The reason behind this name lies in the fact that, as one approaches Dammen, it seems as though there cannot possibly be a way through. From the steep mountain-sides on the left of the fjord, there are two large glaciers which approach each other at right angles and then flow side by side down the mountain and out into the fjord. It looks like an endlessly slow race between the two; a race to be the first to reach the other side of the fjord. They merge into a single body of ice and form a wall across the fjord in front of Dammen, leaving only a 300-400 metre wide channel between the glacier snout and the mountains on the right hand side.

In blinding sunlight, we pass through this channel and at the same time the speed of the wind picks up. Strangely, it feels warm in spite of its strength, though the reason soon becomes clear; it is one of nature's little whims — the Föhn wind.

As we continue towards the head of Dammen, it feels more and more as though a gigantic heater has been turned on somewhere on the icecap where the Föhn is coming from. Wholly unused to such warmth, we soon begin to sweat and our heavy hats are thrown into the sledge bag. We check the thermometer at frequent intervals and find that, in a couple of hours, the temperature has risen from minus 19°C to minus 1°C. The mild weather and the magnificent surroundings, with dazzling white snow and deep blue shadows, bring on a feeling of spring fever.

Once we have reached the end of Dammen and can go no further, we park the dogs and sledge at the edge of Spærregletscher and continue along the glacier edge on foot. Our aim is to see if we can get any further over towards Fure Sø, but we cannot; Spærregletscher lives up to its name (spærre means 'a blockage').

Climbing back down to the dogs, what better place to camp than where we are? For the first time on this spring journey, we can make camp easily, even lazily. I have the outside job and in the mild weather, I can take more time than usual to talk to the dogs. I can also take some photos of the surroundings, knowing that it will be a long while before I see anything like this again. I quite forget the time until Tavsur sticks his head out of the tent and asks if I want to eat soon. A mug of juice stands ready and as I raise it to slake my thirst, I hear a faint noise from the mug. Tavsur has, unknown to me, taken some small pieces of ice from the glacier to put in the drink and as it melts, the small bubbles of air compressed within the ice are released with a hissing, sparkling noise. I take a good swig and feel sorry for all the unlucky people who have never experienced Alpefjord or slaked their thirst with a juice drink chilled with thousand-year-old, crystal-clear glacier ice.

The Föhn wind is still blowing next morning as we head out of Dammen. Surprisingly, the temperature continues to rise and when we have a long break at noon to enjoy the weather and the views, we can sit in shirtsleeves. It is hard to believe, but the temperature has risen to plus 14°C; it is March 17, and, who knows, perhaps at home in Denmark they are still having frost?

Only a faint breeze is blowing now. Sitting in the sunshine for an hour or perhaps more, we can enjoy the warmth and the sight of snow flurries rolling like clouds down the glacier, blown by the Föhn wind. It is a fairytale experience and one could easily wish to linger the rest of the day here, but we have to push on. The dogs are panting because of the warmth and we are forced to go quite slowly in the slushy snow which sticks to our skis; everything has to have a down side. By evening, when we have left Dammen some way behind us, the temperature begins to fall a little but the whole night it stays above plus 8°C and we toss and turn, too warm in our big sleeping bags.

The next morning the Föhn wind disappears as suddenly as it came and the temperature falls to minus15°C, more normal for March and more comfortable for sledge dogs pulling a heavy load.

An unexpected gift

It was back on my first spring journey, on what had been an altogether miserable day. In fact, things had started to go pear-shaped the evening before, as we put up our camp at the head of Røde Sanddal (Red Sand Valley), which links Centrum Sø with Nioghalvfjerdsfjorden.

Tired, I crawled into the tent where a warm mug of cocoa stood ready; just the thing I needed. I slumped down on my sleeping bag, oh, what was that? Ah, I had sat on my diary which I kept in my sleeping bag to protect it when travelling. I turned over to get it out, but as I turned back again I knocked over the full mug of cocoa standing on the food box.

Hell and damnation! The brimful mug went right into my open sleeping bag and the cocoa instantly spread out into a large slushy puddle. I stared aghast at this sludge and at the empty mug while I tried to ignore my partner's enthusiastic applause. If only it had been anything other than this sticky mess; and a whole mug-full. Now I wouldn't even get my warm drink which I had been looking forward to for the last couple of hours. During the past two months, since we left Romer Sø, we had used up all our reserves of body fats and our craving for sweet things had increased dramatically. We had, without exaggeration, been working like donkeys and had ground our way along one stony river bed after another or, where there weren't stones, struggled through deep loose snow. For five whole weeks we had been sledging on land, uphill, downhill, shouting, pushing, yelling, shouting, pushing and so on, while six-weeks-old sweat dripped off us.

A simple calculation showed that our sweat would probably be twice as old by the time we reached Danmarkshavn where we could expect to find a cabin with a shower; there was at least one month's travelling still to go. Now, to complete my discomfort, a mugful of cocoa in my sleeping bag. Whatever next! It had to be dried out, but it would be as sticky as flypaper to sleep in.

That was the way things had gone the previous evening and today was not much of an improvement either, since we had only managed to cover 13 km. Again, we had been pushing hard through stony ground, being forced in several places to unload the sledge and carry the load ahead. At the end of it all, we were lost in a chaos of river channels and hills. We had a map, but with such a large contour interval that it did not show up the small hills we were now camped among, and we had to spend the evening making a reconnaissance on foot to find a way forward.

It was with these thoughts that I sat in the tent, getting the radio ready, when my partner, who had gone outside on some errand or other, shouted excitedly: "Hey, come on out quick, we have got a wolf visitor."

Wolves!

I dropped what I had in my hands and dived out of the tent. Sure enough, 50 metres away from the tent stood two pure white polar wolves. So it had been wolf tracks that we had passed at the head of Danmark Fjord.

We had been driving that day when we came across large dog-like prints near the sledge and had stopped to look more closely. They certainly looked like dog tracks but from an enormous dog with feet about half as big again as Duppen's, and he is no midget.

Could they really be from wolves? We guessed so because there were no loose dogs around.

We took photos but didn't mention it on the radio because, so far as I could remember, the polar wolf had not been seen in Northeast Greenland since the 1930's. Better to wait before letting out the news, in case we were mistaken.

The sight of our two visitors at the camp, watching us apparently without fear, left us without any doubt. There were, once again, polar wolves in Northeast Greenland.

I rummaged feverishly in the tent bag for my camera and put on the telephoto lens, hoping against hope that the wolves would not run away before we could get proof of our observations. Unfortunately, I only got a couple of shots before the wolves became scared by my partner throwing some dog pemmican towards them and they disappeared as silently as they had arrived. We had been so busy with all this that we had not realised that Sirius were trying to contact us on the radio.

"Sirius calling sledge team two, come in sledge team two," sounded from inside the tent.

We hurried in to give our position report and, of course, the reason for our delay in answering. "Wolves?" came over the radio, "Ha, ha, you have been too long in the wilderness. Have you tried counting your dogs?"

We didn't bother to argue, but looked forward eagerly to the time when we would be able to put our pictures on the table in front of the doubters' noses.

It was to be the first and last time I saw wolves, even though we came across their tracks again on a couple of occasions in the following week. Then, one evening almost 14 days later, we heard on the radio from another sledge team, also in North Greenland:

"Hello Sirius. We must agree with sledge team two, because today we also have seen two polar wolves."

Even though there were now two teams agreed on the claim, the last sceptics did not come round to believing us until our photos were developed and displayed in front of their faces back at Daneborg.

The following year, wolf sightings became more common at various places in North and Northeast Greenland: Harald Moltke, Danmarkshavn and even as far south as Loch Fyne. It has since become clear that the polar wolf, after only sporadic roaming to Greenland (from Canada) for about 40 years, has in fact returned to Northeast Greenland to stay and breed. It was, really, a fantastic experience for me to witness their return; my bad humour resulting from the spilt cocoa evaporated. I felt as if I had been given an unexpected present. The day we saw the wolves was my birthday!

Spring

Now it is April, and May is not far ahead.

The dark time? It is just a memory. Advancing with giant strides by 20 minutes every day, the daylight lengthens and the sun is winning its battle. Our faces become more sunburnt and it is plain to see that it is no longer the bitter cold wind that burns us. Day after day we become browner on the face and neck, with a sharp line of contrast along our shirt collars between sunburnt skin and the whiteness of the rest of our clothed bodies.

Just as seeing the sun again after the dark time warms the heart, the middle of April brings a similar joy; the sound of the first snow bunting.

There is nothing special about this bird-song; the snow bunting is only the polar cousin of the common sparrow, but when one has not heard any small bird song for over half a year, the snow bunting's piping whistle sounds really beautiful. We look around to find the source of the sound.

"There he is," I say to my partner, as much as anything to convince myself that it is really true. The dogs carry their heads higher, breaking into a gallop sometimes and even though one sparrow does not make a spring in these surroundings, the new season seems to start from this moment.

As the days pass, snow buntings follow in small flocks of five or ten and in the wake of these harbingers of summer, the other migrant birds follow little by little. Plovers, turnstones, sandpipers, terns, eider ducks, and barnacle geese to name but a few. In not much more than a month, they have all arrived. We keep a count from the sledge of the new arrivals, noting which types and how many of each pass over us.

Soon after the first snow buntings have flown in from the south, the sun ceases to set and stays above the horizon all night. The midnight sun has arrived, snow and cold are now in full retreat and we turn to a night-time sledging routine. In the autumn, we changed to the night for a while to use the light of the full moon, but now the change to night-time travelling is because during the day, in the powerful high-arctic sunlight, the daytime temperature can easily climb several degrees above freezing, making the snow slushy and slow. The dogs, with their heavy coats, prefer the cool of the night for working. They enjoy, like we do too, sitting in the afternoon sun in the free time between two nights of travel. As a rule, we take down the tent in the evening when the temperature has fallen to five or ten degrees below freezing. Then, in the cool of the night, we travel until well into the morning, depending on conditions and how far we want to go.

The sun does not always follow the rules and just as we begin to think of enjoying sun and warmth every day, there can come a snowstorm at least as violent as anything we get in the winter. Even at midsummer, earth and sky can become one in a blinding blizzard. What the weather and the wind also determine is that other characteristic of spring; fog which, on windless days, can hang like a wet blanket over the whole area of the outer coast. Then all navigation has to be by compass. In spite of these drawbacks, April and May are the most pleasant months for sledge travel; the snow conditions are still good enough and the wildlife is returning.

Another sign of early spring is the first small melt stream. Even though it is sweet to hear through the tent walls the sound of running water, when everything has been frost-bound and silent for so long, it is also a reminder that it is time to set a course for home. Melt water is nice to listen to, but not half as attractive to travel through with a dog sledge.

Tavsur and I went a long way south in the spring of 1979, so we were certainly the first to see a melt river that year. It was as early as 2 April, exactly the day when we so to speak, marked with our sledge tracks the southern boundary of our patrol area.

We were travelling in Jameson and Liverpool Lands, about one good day's travel north of Scoresbysund with its resident

Greenlandic population when, for two days, we were held up by bad weather in a place called Klitdal, the southerly extension of Carlsberg Fjord.

The blizzard hit us with a violence that forced us to camp before we reached Store Fjord which was our target for the day. We had already made good 43 km in six hours when we saw that something was blowing up. We tried to get out of the north- south trending valley of Klitdal but didn't manage it because the rising wind picked up so much drifting snow, reducing visibility drastically; we decided to camp before the situation became critical.

For two whole days we lay inactive in our sleeping bags and listened to the roaring of the storm and the violent flapping of the tent. Outside, the visibility remained less than five metres. It was hard to guess the wind speed but we were certainly glad that we had built a wall of snow blocks around the tent to deflect the worst of the storm. That snow wall gave us quite a surprise when, on the second day of the storm and just as the wind was reaching a climax, it blew over onto the tent. Luckily there were no serious consequences other than forcing us to get out quickly and rebuild it.

Each day, as usual, we reported our position to Sirius and it was on the second day of this storm that we managed to send birthday greetings over the radio to one of our comrades who was celebrating his 25th birthday at Kap Morris Jesup — the most northerly point of land in Greenland and in the whole world, 1400 km as the crow flies, from our own camp. (The world's most northerly land is in fact a small gravel bank, Odak Ø, which is in the Polar Sea about one km from Kap Morris Jesup.)

As an illustration of just how big an area the patrol covered, a third sledge team was on the westerly corner of North Greenland at exactly this same time, barely 100 km from Ellesmere Island in Canada.

One month later, during a night in early May, we are on our tortuous route northwards and homewards towards Daneborg, heading towards Bontekoe, an island in Foster Bugt near the mouth of Kejser Franz Joseph Fjord.

It is quite an ordinary spring night and while the island slowly and almost imperceptibly rises above the horizon and grows bigger as we approach, we can from time to time, see dark dots on the sea ice in front of us. We rub our eyes to make sure — yes, there is another over there. Seals! Several of them have come up right on our course but they are wary and we seldom get closer than 200 metres before they sense us and disappear through their breathing holes to reach safety beneath the metre-thick ice.

We enjoy seeing the wildlife around us during the night. When everything goes like a well-oiled machine and the dogs with their steaming breath, run well in an orderly five or six-metre broad fan formation, the animals and birds we see along the way give us a refreshing change which we can hardly fail to enjoy. They are often a source of surprise and wonder too; for example, the muskoxen that we meet the next day on Bontekoe, as we are on a walking trip over the island.

Suddenly, there they stand; two muskoxen. Why in the world they have come to wander out to Bontekoe, 30 km from the nearest mainland, is hard to understand. They seem alright, well fed in fact, and hardly bother to give us a look as we pass by.

Muskoxen are unpredictable in several ways; one day they can be seen grazing in herds and then, the next day at the same place, there may be not a single animal to be seen. I remember clearly on my first autumn journey, as we passed over Albrechtsletten on Wollaston Forland, how it looked like an old photograph of an American prairie. Large herds, not of bison obviously but of the similar-looking muskox. How many there were on the Albrechtsletten that day I do not know, but we actually counted 218.

On my last spring journey we counted the total number of muskoxen we had seen during our four months of travelling and it came to 847 animals. The total number living in Northeast Greenland would be hard to guess.

It is not only muskox that we meet on Bontekoe. We also see a female bear with her two cubs, walking over a small hilltop. This is no great surprise for us because, with such an abundance of seals down on the sea ice, there are bound to be polar bears around. In the last four days alone, we have seen seven bears, five adults and two young cubs. Even so, we stop to enjoy the sight of this bear family until it disappears from sight.

From Bontekoe, we continue our journey and on 17 May, arrive at Myggbukta, the main Norwegian trapping station in the old days. It is only a coincidence that we arrive here on the Norwegian National Day but, at the same time, our arrival is planned because we have heard well in advance over the radio, that a Swedish ornithological expedition expects to arrive at Myggbukta on that day. We aim to say hello to them.

The expedition, The Swedish Northeast Greenland Expedition 1979 to give it its full name, consisting of Magnus Elander and Sven Blomquist, finally arrived from Mestersvig with snow scooters on 18 May. Since Tavsur and I still had some time in hand for the rest of our patrol, we stayed an extra day at Myggbukta to help the Swedes, a couple of cheerful guys, to settle in.

It was from here at Myggbukta that, in 1931, some Norwegian hunters were in a position to stir up the controversy between Norway and Denmark by 'occupying' a large area of Northeast Greenland and claiming it as Norwegian territory — Erik Raudes Land they called it.

Fortunately the two countries came to their senses and allowed the International Court at The Hague to decide the matter. It all ended to Denmark's advantage, but with a rebuke to Denmark that they should show their flag a little more often; one of the most important reasons behind the continued existence of the Sirius Patrol.

The Sledge Tracks end

Tavsur and I got back from our spring journey relatively early in 1979. There were several reasons for this but it was mainly due to good luck with the weather, the travelling conditions and the dogs.

We reached the hut at Dahl Skær on 25 May, only a short day's journey south of Daneborg.

Arriving in excellent humour thanks to the dogs who had, for the last few days, surpassed themselves, we had also had several strokes of good luck. For instance the day before, when we were cleaning up the hut at Eskimonæs.

In the middle of our labours, there was a sudden commotion amongst the dogs and so I stuck my head out of the hut door to see what was the matter and realised that we had guests. In fact, barely 50 metres from the hut stood a large male bear, looking at us with a mixture of curiosity and alarm. Through the camera lens, one could practically see the two emotions battling inside him. Seemingly they were well balanced because he stayed there without moving for about ten minutes, until he could no longer stand the racket made by the dogs. By this time we had taken several rolls of film, so we parted the best of friends as he calmly and peacefully made his way back onto the ice at Gael Hamkes Bugt.

Throughout the entire spring journey, we had kept to a rule that we would make any small detours necessary to visit sights of interest that lay along our route. If, for example, there was an old hunter's hut that we hadn't seen before, we would head for it and look around. Of course, we had to see the old eskimo ruins at Breivik and Dødemandsbugten (Dead Man's Bay) during our tour from Eskimonæs to Dahl Skær. At Dødemandsbugten we could see the remnants of the fortifications left by our predecessors, *Nordøstgrønlands Slædepatrulje* (Northeast Greenland's Sledge Patrol) who had built them as a defence against Germans during the Second World War. This detour added 31 km and took us four and a half hours; in spite of the fact that it was the 109th day of our trip, we travelled very fast!

Talking about days and distances, as we sat in Dahl Skær hut and Tavsur, for the last time, served juice, liver paste and tuna in tomato sauce, I looked for my diary, paper and pencil and calculated some distances. Our tape player was at full volume, using the last of our batteries to play old tunes, and the dogs were happily eating an extra ration of dried fish out in the sunshine.

What I managed to calculate was that I had covered more than 7,700 km in the 337 days that I had been sledging. Not all the days had been travelling days, of course, due to bad weather and waiting around. All the same, it sounded impressive to me. I did not brag to Tavsur, who had already passed the 10,000 km mark and still wanted to do a fourth season as a patrol man; anyway, all my comrades would have much the same figures to show.

I lay back on the bunk and thought about it all. It was hard to appreciate that the sledging tomorrow would most probably be the last for me, on this tour at least. To be completely honest, I could not deny that there had been times when I had looked forward to this moment, but I felt sad now that the end was in sight. Even though there had been grey days and downright bad days, I had never experienced such a total sense of freedom as on these sledge journeys.

So many memories came back to me lying there on my bunk, such as the occasion when we jumped over the melt water crack at Kap David Gray and I took an involuntary ducking in Hochstetterbugten, or the time the sledge slid away from us in Promenadedal and went over a 50 metre high cliff, miraculously collecting only superficial damage. We had certainly had our share of good luck.

So far as thin ice is concerned, I still remember with a shudder a day in May 1978, when we were travelling up into Søndre Mellemland. That was on my first spring journey when, together with other Sirius men, we had been flown to North Greenland. At the beginning of May, my partner and I were on our way south, although not directly, for we had instructions to investigate some of the hinterland on our way along the coast. Among other places, we were instructed to go up to Sæl Sø and Anneks Sø, west of Germanialand, but before we got that far we were to make a detour into an un-named fjord in the area called Søndre

Mellemland. 'Drive carefully' had been written into our instructions, and the reason for the warning was only too clear afterwards.

After five or six hours travelling through the morning, we approached Søndre Mellemland from the northeast. The weather was fine and the previous night had passed without any noteworthy events.

Just before we reached the mouth of the fjord, the ice abruptly changed in character. The old snow-covered sea ice that we had been driving on in Jøkelbugten, came to an end and we had to climb up a couple of metres or so onto what most closely resembled a layer of newly frozen autumn ice. It was not a nice place. At the step up, we could hear water rushing underneath us, presumably due to a strong current. As if that was not enough, there was a thin layer of snow on top of the ice but a number of bare patches round about where the snow had disappeared because of water coming up through holes in the ice. It all looked rather strange but we thought that if we took care to travel on the snowy portions, we could probably avoid any holes; there were only about two km to go before we would reach land.

All went well, we reached the land safely and while I put up the tent and fed the dogs, my partner went further up the fjord to scout around. He returned unexpectedly quickly with the information that we could not go any further because of open water.

This meant that we had no alternative but to go back out to the solid ice in Jøkelbugten once again. That would probably have gone easily enough but for the unlucky fact that the wind got up during the night. Where did that leave us? Well, the next morning when we looked out towards the mouth of the fjord, the thin layer of snow that had helped us avoid the thin ice patches had disappeared; blown away. This was not good news since neither of us had any wish to find out how deep those holes were in the ice; nevertheless, we had to move and we decided to go ahead, trusting to the dogs' sensitivity and instinct when crossing dangerous ice and hoping for a little luck.

Those two to three km out to the thick safe ice were something I shall not forget. We found that the ice surface was now polished smooth and there was a slight tail-wind so that the dogs had no difficulty in pulling the sledge, but their feet broke through several times and the sledge runners did the same, making it a nerve-racking time. The sledge left two ruts behind it where the water was coming up from below; it was simply our speed that was keeping us on the surface.

By now, we had jumped onto the sledge and were yelling and shouting at the dogs to keep going at full speed; not really necessary when they were undoubtedly as worried as ourselves.

How much time it took before we were out on the safe ice again I just don't know, but it was certainly a nice feeling when we could get off the sledge and put our skis down onto a solid surface.

One month later we did get a wetting and it happened as a result of such a stupid accident.

We were on our way out to Shannon Ø and intended to pass by Kap David Gray and over to Kuhn Ø. It was around the beginning of June, and by this time of the year there are often leads (long splits) starting to form in the sea ice and fjord ice. These are usually not a big problem, only one or two metres wide, and the dogs know how to deal with them. If we see that we agree approaching a lead, we shout '*revne, revne, revne*' (*revne* meaning 'crack') and the dogs speed up to a flat-out gallop. From full speed, they stop right at the edge of the lead and wait a second for the sledge to run up behind them and almost push them into the water. At exactly the right moment, with enough slack in their traces, they leap to the other side of the lead and keep going. The momentum of the sledge enables it to bump over the gap, while we hop onto either side of it to get a ride over the water. The whole procedure was normally nothing to worry about and much less complicated to do than to describe!

The rule of thumb was that leads with a width less than the length of the sledge, say up to about three metres, could be crossed without much problem but, if things should go wrong, there was no real danger to life and limb since one could always get a grip on the edge of the ice. It was a different matter altogether with thin ice or wider leads, and much more dangerous. Not many people want to take a bath in water at freezing point, even though they have not had a wash for a couple of months.

We knew well enough about the lead out by Kap David Gray. I had seen it earlier in the season when, one fine sunny day, I had taken a trip out there with a camera. There were always a lot of birds to be seen in the area. On that occasion, I had gone as far as the cape so that I could see the mainland and take a compass bearing to Kuhn Ø in case the fog came down. As I stood there, I could see the lead running right in to land and stretching as far southwards as I could see. Close to the land the lead was only a metre or so wide, but it became wider away from the shore. When I got back, I mentioned this finding.

Everything went well on the evening in question, until we rounded the cape and had to pass this lead.

"Hey, should we not turn in close to the shore where it is narrowest?" I shouted, but we didn't because the old hand yelled '*revne, revne, revne*' at full volume and the dogs charged ahead.

A second or two before we reached the edge of the lead, it became clear to both of us that this was going to go wrong. We loosened our grip on the sledge and braked as hard as we could with our skis.

Splash!

Half the dogs didn't make it and were swimming in the water but the lead was exactly the width that allowed the front of the sledge together with the rest of the dogs to reach the other side while the back end of the sledge was hanging down into the icy cold waters of Hochstetterbugt.

"Jump across to the other side and pull the sledge," yelled the old hand.

There wasn't much point in speculating, so I took a run and jumped. Splash! My run had been too short and I sank to my head before I got myself out on the other side. A few more moments and we had the sledge and the other dogs out too.

"I thought you said the lead was only one metre wide," said the old hand.

"Yes, down close to the shore," I said, pointing. It hung in the air between us for some time, that we each had our own opinion about who had screwed up on this, but what was done was done and there are times when it is not worth arguing. I took my ski poles and ran ahead the rest of the way to try to keep warm in my soaking wet clothes and to get more speed from the dogs. We reached Kuhn Ø without further mishap and, as it turned out, not much water had got into the two sledge boxes on the back of the sledge. There was no other damage and luckily it was only about two degrees below freezing that night. At least I had no worries about catching a cold; germs are one thing that we did not have to think about in the isolation and the cold dry air of Northeast Greenland.

That kind of swim is something most Sirius men have to experience sooner or later, before their two seasons are out. On the day when Tavsur and I arrived at Dahl Skær, there was another sledge team far to the north at Centrum Sø who seemed to be swimming the rest of their way back to Daneborg and who broke all the records for late homecoming from a spring journey. It was the same sledge team that had perhaps tempted fate by calling their sledge *Ra*! (Thor Heyerdahl's raft). Whether or not it was this challenge to fate that decided it, I do not know but their patrol journey was delayed so much by poor travelling conditions that spring-time caught up with them on their southward journey. They had a month of serious difficulties racing the onset of summer; in spite of meltwater rivers and leads in the sea ice, they managed to make their way back to arrive at Albrechtsletten as late as 23 June, mid summer; an impressive achievement for which all the other Sirius people gave them full credit.

We followed their progress over the radio with mounting excitement and as soon as we heard that they had made it to land not far from Daneborg, a rescue team of four men left to help them and their dogs on the last leg home. *Ra*, the sledge, had to be left at Albrechtsletten but was brought home later in the summer by helicopter.

That epic was still one month in the future as we lay at Dahl Skær and listened to Eric Clapton for the 117th time. It was idyllic but, nicotine poisoned wreck that I was, I was longing for a cigarette. I had smoked my last a week earlier and Tavsur had also finished his supply — or so he said.

He went outside for a moment but returned with a grin, waving something or other. "There," he said triumphantly.

He had in fact saved his last packet so that we could share them on our last sledging day. What a partner!

Later that evening, as the brilliant arctic sun shone down on us, we loaded the sledge for the last time and headed up through Henning Elv and then down to Young Sund.

Just before driving down onto the fjord ice and home to our comrades on the base, we paused and gazed in silence towards Daneborg, where the sledge tracks had to end.

7. JUNE AND JULY

From dog sledge to patrol boat

By the middle of June, night frosts at Daneborg are a thing of the past and the thaw sets in seriously. Sounds of melting and running water are everywhere and day by day, the amount of snow lying about the place decreases.

This season of thaw is a pleasant time provided everyone has returned safely from their sledge journeys. It is good to see all the others again, some of them barely recognisable, being so sunburnt and having lost so much weight. Some are hiding behind shaggy beards and hair though most of us attack it with scissors the first day after we arrive back at the station. There is a lot of talk about the sledge journeys and when all are safely back, there is of course a good old-fashioned Sirius lunch; the midsummer party.

This early summer period is used for many activities. The first job always, after returning to Daneborg, is to see that all the sledge equipment is repaired, cleaned and put away. After that, there is usually a week or so to be spent indoors, writing reports about the spring sledge journey. Outside, the time is used to paint and tar the huts and, down by the fjord, the boats have to be made ready for the coming summer season. In no time at all, it is the middle of July and the new team of Sirius recruits arrives, dressed in their spotless dark blue working clothes; another year is past and the cycle starts all over again. This brings it home to some of us that we have already been here for two years; a few have become three-years men or one of the old 'burnt-out' guys, as they are called, for whom it will be good to get south once again.

In this way, my story might end were it not for something called summer residence at Ella Ø, an important part of the tour of duty. I understand fully why many before me have said that this summer period at Ella Ø was the best of all. For me too, the obligatory Ella Ø sojourn was the most memorable, especially since it was also the last part of my spell as a Sirius man.

I remember clearly the evening of 21 July 1979. There was not a cloud in the sky and not a breath of wind. Young Sund was like a mirror. Those of us going to Ella Ø were assured that, when we flew there the next day, it would also be our final departure from and farewell to Daneborg, the place that for two years had become our home and to which we had formed a strong attachment.

I decided to take a last tour round the station, past the harbour where my possessions were lying already packed in two containers, and finishing at my dog team. One last time I went round and talked with them and now I stood and watched them as they lay down again in unworried fashion.

As I lingered there a few more moments, enjoying the company of my dogs and the views of the mountains and their reflections in the fjord, I realised for the first time that something had happened to me during the course of these two years. Even though I would soon be on my way home to Denmark, my life would never feel quite the same again.

8. SUMMER ON ELLA Ø

We are on our way from Daneborg to Ella Ø in a GLACE helicopter. Besides the pilot and mechanic, there are five of us Sirius men on board; two novices, two old hands and one veteran. The veteran is Henrik Friis, who was attached to the patrol for a number of years in the 1960s and early '70s.

We five have the task of manning Ella Ø for the summer with responsibility for re-supply and repairs to the depots and the huts in the area that we can approach from the water, using Ella Ø as our base. This task extends to all the depots that lie in the fjord complex between Moskusoksefjord in the north and Kong Oscar Fjord in the south.

It is fine flying weather, with visibility limited only by the horizon and the mountains. Throughout the flight, we gaze eagerly out of the windows, partly to get an idea of the sailing conditions but also to admire the landscape spread out beneath us. It is strange to see the whole area with a bird's eye perspective, the fjords and places that we came to know from weeks of sledge travel, now seen again as a rapid flash back during the hour it takes for the flight

"Down there is such and such hut ... there we saw a bear ... there we were stuck in bad weather ... think, we used a whole day to get through that valley."

Passing over Ymer Ø there, right in front of us lies Ella Ø, a mountain massif with steep sides that rise almost vertically out of Kempe Fjord. Half way along its northwestern flank, there is a small peninsula on which lies the station.

In only a few minutes we are on our way down and the Norwegian pilot is circling round once to give the photographers a view. Even from up here it looks a fine place. The red-painted wooden huts with black tarred roofs make the station look like a neat Scandinavian village.

We land, and even though it is evening, the air is warm; a completely different feel to what we have become used to at Daneborg where it can be mild but seldom to the extent that one wants to take one's shirt off. There is a natural explanation for this in that Daneborg lies close to the outer coast where there is nearly always a cool breeze, but here on Ella Ø, 100 km further in towards the mainland, it is absolutely calm.

A green and fertile place it seems to us old hands, used as we are to Northeast Greenland's humble vegetation; and what a situation the station has! It feels almost as though nature planned in advance that people would be able to make this a place to live. There is a fresh water lake only two hundred metres from the station, to supply fresh running water. There is an anchorage out in a small rock-free bay where there is always shelter from wind and drift ice. As if that is not enough, there is an absolute feast for the eyes. Wherever one looks there are views of splendid mountain ranges and, behind the station,The Bastion rises to over 1000 metres in an absolutely vertical wall.

Dr Lauge Koch surely understood the advantage of combining pleasure with practical necessity when he, in his time (1926), founded the Ella Ø station as the main base for his scientific (geological) investigations in Kong Christian X's Land. One begins to understand why Ella Ø is called the 'Pearl of the East Coast' and, for anyone who has already been captivated by Northeast Greenland, Ella Ø feels something like a Garden of Eden. However, just as there was a snake to spoil the idyllic perfection of that place, it does not take long to discover that this paradise in Greenland has its equivalent; we are scarcely out of the plane before a horde of huge bloodthirsty mosquitoes, the worst plague of the tundra lands, swarms all over us. We had no such pests at Daneborg. Still, mosquitoes or not, Ella Ø looks like living up to our high expectations. Once the helicopter has been unloaded and sent on its way to Mestersvig, we stand for a while and let our senses absorb the silence and the view, before we hoist the Dannebrog (the national flag of Denmark) as a sign that Ella Ø is, once again, occupied.

Next day, we start on our tasks. First of all, one of the patrol boats must be made ready for sea. *Britt*, as the cutter is called, is sitting on its bogie, covered with tarpaulins since the last season as a protection against the wind and weather.

This 22-foot cutter is unwrapped and given an overhaul both inside and out. The motor is looked over and given fresh oil, the batteries re-charged and a new layer of white and red paint added to the well preserved, ice-sheathed hull.

An improvement compared to Daneborg is that we do not have to haul the cutter out onto land between depot trips to avoid the danger of drifting pack ice, and there is also a floating pontoon which we can put out and use whenever we have to load *Britt.*

After several days of work, stripped to the waist in a temperature of plus 20°C in the shade, both *Britt* and the pontoon are lying ready in the water and we can start the depot trips.

Three men sail away while the other two set about repairs to the station and getting supplies ready for the next boat trip; the crews will then be reversed so that everyone has an equal share of the boating.

Nine tins of fish, 12 tins of liver paste and six tins of main meal; a new Sirius guy and I, who are left behind, are gathering together supplies.

I stand with a handful of sheets of paper covered with notes detailing which supplies must go to the different depots. The lists were prepared for us beforehand at Daneborg by a triumvirate consisting of the Provisions man, the Nordre man and the Dog man. As I read the lists and tick off the items one by one, the new hand finds them and packs them into the strong steel boxes which, with a bit of luck, will stand up to attacks by polar bears.

We must pack for five or six depots which we will visit on our next trip and once everything is in order, we carry the steel boxes down to the pontoon. After that, more trips with dog food such as dried fish, dog pemmican and pork fat, to stock up the dog food huts. Once we have collected all the man and dog provisions, we must also roll down to the shore five barrels of paraffin and carry down 13 sacks of coal. To finish with, we assemble all the hardware that may be needed, such as skis, ski sticks, hut lamps, matches, toilet paper and a mass of other smaller and larger things. We write addresses on everything and then gather together all the materials that we shall have to use to repair damaged huts; wood, roofing felt, plexiglas and so on.

It takes us a day to get everything organised, but *Britt* will be away for at least two more days yet, so we decide that we can have a day off; what a place for a free day! We can take a walk up past the lakes which lie like giant steps leading up to the mountains. There is masses of wildlife higher up and there are almost certain to be muskox. With five or six hours to spare, it is possible for us to continue further up onto The Bastion; a truly magnificent walk on such a clear day. It is a dizzying experience to stand at the top of these cliffs and look over the edge, vertically down into the deep blue water of Kempe Fjord where the mighty icebergs look like small white spots. It is possible to see many miles along the length of Kong Oscar Fjord and all the way to Kap Wardlew, 170 km distant; fantastic to think that from this point, one is looking at an area nearly the size of Denmark.

At Daneborg, arctic foxes were scarce visitors because the dogs' presence usually scared them away, but on the first day after our arrival at Ella Ø, we have a visit from a curious fox cub which we promptly christen Thorkild. After a quarter of an hour, he has already learned to eat out of our hands. Even though Thorkild will not allow us to touch him, he seems to have no fear of us and he makes himself at home on the station without further ado. From that day, he is counted as a member of the family.

If it is an unforgettable experience to travel in Northeast Greenland with a dog sledge in wintertime, it is no less exciting to travel along the fjords in perfect weather in the summertime.

Everything seems so clean and fresh and when we pass one of the numerous icebergs, we can see just how crystal clear the deep water is. Going close by allows us to see how the huge blue-green mass of ice disappears many metres down into the dark depths.

There are icebergs of all sizes ranging from small lumps, which the boat easily pushes aside, right up to enormous colossi measuring hundreds of metres across and standing ten stories high above the water. These monsters, as well as most lesser icebergs, we keep well clear of since, although the melting may be minimal, it is well known that an iceberg can eventually become unbalanced and turn over without warning. Titanic forces are let loose in such a capsize, with several-metre-high waves forming; lumps of ice the size of a house can break off the berg underwater and come shooting up to the surface with unbelievable force.

We change places at the tiller every couple of hours or so while sailing from one depot to the next. There must always be two men on deck since, even if we wear lifejackets, there would be no hope of surviving more than a couple of minutes in the ice cold water if anyone fell in unobserved.

We do not make any distinction between day and night on these boat trips; we just eat when we are hungry, work when there is work to be done and sleep when we get so tired that we can do nothing else; a splendid way to live (plate 13).

With the motor at its slowest speed we approach the shore. One man stands in the bow and watches for rocks beneath the surface. Quite quickly, the water changes colour, the sea bed rises up into sight and there is a shout from the bow. The boathook is pushed down to measure the depth, a couple of metres being what we need to allow for tidal ebb. At a signal from the bow-man, the propeller is put into reverse and the anchor dropped.

Looking in towards land, we can see that the hut door is standing open; a sure sign that a bear has been visiting. Pulling the dinghy alongside, we load it with supplies and take a quick run in to the beach and up to the hut. Things are not in as bad a state as they might be; only the outer door and the window are smashed. However, one end wall of the hut obviously needs a new layer of felt and so one man goes back to the cutter to fetch the necessary tools and materials.

Depending on the condition of the depot, we may spend anything from one hour to a whole day at the place, but by the time we are finished, everything is as new again, with fresh supplies of all the provisions needed.

Every item of food and equipment is recorded so that the sledge teams on their autumn journey will know what was left in the depot. Before closing the door and window behind us, we also write a short greeting in the hut book and wish future visitors 'Good luck from *Britt* and her crew.'

As the days and the summer pass, one depot trip follows another and every day, we talk on the radio with the operator at Daneborg to exchange news and hear how their work progresses. The winter's sledging programme depends very much on the new supplies taken out by boat and we feel sad in a way that we will not be the ones to use these depots or enjoy the improvements, but that is the way it is. After all, we have already used and enjoyed the depots provided by the previous year's team.

Fresh supplies are also brought to Ella Ø itself and on one of the first days in August, *Thala Dan* anchors in the bay. The day of the annual ship's visit stands out as the usual burst of frantic activity. All of a sudden there is a crowd of people. Tourists, who have chosen to spend a summer holiday travelling with a polar ship, swarm ashore to take photographs. We come to feel a bit like rare animals in a zoo, as the tourists use one roll of film after another to record these strange people who have volunteered for exile in this god-forsaken place.

Thala Dan is not the only ship to visit Ella Ø during the summer. Over the radio we are told that a French boat has come through the Storis (the huge and more or less permanent pack-ice belt along Northeast Greenland's coast), so it does not come as a complete surprise when, one evening in the middle of August, we see the Tricolor flying over a red-painted boat on course for the station. *Vagabond II*, which this 15 metre yacht is called, turns out to be under the command of the owner, a French engineer, who has always wanted to visit Northeast Greenland; often a risky business, as several other sailors have come to realise over the years. The Storis is not a joke and, in the summer of '77 for example, two Norwegian yachts were crushed when attempting to get back to the open ocean after visiting the coast.

Because of poor weather, *Vagabond II* and its seven-man crew decide to stay at Ella Ø for a couple of days, and the Frenchmen are sensible enough to think carefully before going all the way up to Daneborg. Weather conditions suggest that they may be better advised to set a course towards the Greenland Sea again and we later hear that they have in fact reached the open ocean safely.

On one of the last days in August, as we are heading home from a depot trip in Kong Oscars Fjord, something red catches our attention on the shore near the Kap Elisabeth hut. Turning *Britt* about, we head in to see what it is.

Approaching the land, we can see that the red is a sleeping bag lying on the shore. A watcher comes out of the hut and as we approach, we gather that he is English. He explains that he belongs to an expedition that is attempting to climb Petermanns Bjerg. Unluckily, he has injured a foot and has been left behind while his friends continue further in an inflatable boat, intending to collect him on their return journey.

We ask if he wants to come back with us to the station, but he politely declines.

Has he any weapon for his defence? No, he has not.

Then we ask him if he is aware that there can be polar bears in the area. He shakes his head, alarmed, and when we tell him about the bear that we saw a few days ago swimming in the area of Ella Ø, he changes his mind. In only a few minutes he has packed his rucksack together with the red sleeping bag, and is very ready to come with us back to the station. His colleagues, as instructed in the message which we leave on the spot, will come to collect him some days later.

After about ten bad days of windy weather in the middle of August, things improve again towards the end of the month and once again, we can enjoy clear calm evenings. Sitting outside in the evening peace with coffee and a pipe we can, from time to time, hear a deep rumble from further up the fjord, echoing between the mountain walls like distant thunder, as one of the great glaciers calves a new ice berg.

The best moment of all is when, sitting deep in thought, there is a quiet rustling in the gravel alongside. It comes as quite a surprise when this turns out to be a muskox who has come trudging down and, in complete silence as if it was the most natural thing in the world, begun to eat the station's juicy grass only a few metres away from us. Like Thorkild, the muskox becomes a part of life of the station. Every evening at around midnight, Wolfgang Amadeus Bolohni Ohlson, as we name him for some obscure reason, comes calmly down from the mountains, grazes until the early morning and then stoically climbs back up into the mountains again (plate 32).

In spite of the fine weather at the end of August, the summer is clearly coming to an end, the warmth is disappearing from the air and in the mornings, the ground is hard and frozen. Where not so long ago there were areas of green, I can now see only patches of rust-red and brown.

At the station we contemplate the coming autumn without anxiety, since all the depot trips have been successfully completed and by 1 September we have finished our tasks; we have only to take *Britt* out of the water and make the station ready for winter. This is left to the three old hands while the two new Sirius men are flown up to their new home at Daneborg. The three of us left behind are told we will be picked up on 5 September to be taken to Mestersvig and from there we, together with all other homeward-bound personnel, will continue south to Denmark.

Even though we are finished with the official boating journeys, we decide to take one last tour with *Britt*, purely and simply a sightseeing trip across Kempe Fjord to Ørken Dal where the river, every summer for thousands of years, has eroded a deep, narrow gorge into the bedrock with a waterfall running down it. This is the last sight we feel we must see before leaving Ella Ø.

The trip is fantastic, as is the view of The Bastion from this new angle. We take many photos and, as fate would have it, I drop and damage my camera on this very last tour. The camera has been with me on all my sledge and boat journeys, and has worked faultlessly in spite of daily being knocked about, of temperatures down to minus 57°C, and of sledge crashes and salt water spray; now it is out of action. In a remote land such as this, with so many fantastic situations which one is daily wanting to be able to record on film, the camera becomes a personal friend and is in almost constant use.

Yet, as I write these words, I can still see clearly in my mind that afternoon when the helicopter came for us and landed on Ella Ø.

Britt is drawn up on the beach, cleaned and covered over; the windows in the red-painted hut are shuttered up.

The red and white Danish flag has been taken down and we have written a last greeting in the hut book, wishing good weather and good travelling for our successors.

The summer on Ella Ø is over; my time with Sirius is almost over and in silence, we cast a last look back before the helicopter sets a course southwards.

9. HOME FROM SIRIUS

In the afternoon of 7 September 1979, we land at Kastrup airport on the ordinary scheduled flight from Keflavik to Copenhagen.

Home again — well, yes?

Unchanged, is the first impression one gets of things on returning, but words like alien or restlessness soon come to mind.

Theoretically I had set aside, including time spent in training as well as in Greenland, one thousand days from the calendar of that time of my life when my contemporaries found their first foothold in society. In practice, the number of days is considerably greater than that, as a number of Sirius people have come to realise.

Have I any regrets?

No, not for one second; Sirius has been something that I would never have wanted to miss.

When I think of my comrades, both those who travelled north with me in 1977 and those whom I met in Greenland, I am glad and proud to be able to say that I was a Sirius man.

Some people have asked me simply; "What does it feel like returning home from Sirius?"

I really don't know, but I am not certain that I will ever again feel so completely at home as I have for the past two years!

APPENDICES

A. HISTORICAL SUMMARY OF NORTHEAST GREENLAND

Greenland

Geographically Greenland, the largest island in the world, belongs to the North American continent. It has an area of 2.2 million square km, of which four fifths is covered by a permanent ice cap, the so-called 'Inland Ice'. In some places, this ice is as thick as 3.2 km. The population (88% born in Greenland and 12% born outside Greenland) totals 56,000 of which the majority live in southwest Greenland, with fishing, hunting and sheep breeding as their main industries.

A Danish colony since 1721, Greenland became an equal part of Denmark in 1953. In 1979 Greenland obtained Home Rule status within the Unity of the Realm with Denmark and the Faeroe Islands. The Landsting is the parliament of Greenland, and Landsstyret is the cabinet. Nuuk, the largest town in Greenland with 13,500 inhabitants, is the seat of government and lies on the west coast.

Northeast Greenland

The name, Northeast Greenland, usually denotes the coastal area between Scoresby Sund and Nordostrundingen, while the area between Nordostrundingen and Thule is normally called North Greenland. In this book however, the name Northeast Greenland is used a little loosely to refer to the entire area along Greenland's uninhabited coast from Liverpool Land on the east coast to Hall Land on the north coast.

The great belt of pack-ice (the Storis) off the north east coast acts like snow covered land so far as the climate is concerned and the whole area has a high arctic continental climate. It has polar nights and a corresponding summer period with midnight sun lasting approximately three months.

Geologically, Northeast Greenland is like an open book. The bedrock is only covered by a thin layer of soil and low vegetation in low lying areas and by ice to a greater extent. Where seen, however, the rock is fresh and unweathered, having recently been exposed to glaciation. Geological eras represented range from ancient Caledonian gneiss formations, through sandstones and other sedimentary rocks to huge areas of younger, eruptive volcanic rocks, mainly Tertiary in age.

The southern part of the area is home to large herds of muskoxen, the number varying drastically but probably between 5,000 and 15,000 animals. Terrestrial mammals are represented by polar bear, arctic wolf, arctic fox, ermine, alpine hare and collared lemming. Marine mammals such as walrus and various species of whale and seal are common. Throughout the summer, the rivers are rich with char. A large number of migratory birds breed in Northeast Greenland but only snowy owl, gyr falcon, raven and ptarmigan stay for the winter.

North and Northeast Greenland have no native population. The two dozen or so inhabitants on the stations at Mestersvig airfield, Sirius Daneborg, Danmarkshavn, and Station Nord are all Danish.

Discovery of North and Northeast Greenland

The Norsemen

Long before Europeans arrived, the Inuit were the first explorers of the Arctic. Through their daily lives, they travelled and explored huge areas in search of food, supplies and settlement areas. The Inuit came to North and Northeast Greenland from Arctic America around 4,500 years ago. Living conditions were marginal and the Inuit cultures developed and disappeared as changes occurred in the climate and fauna. Their travels remain undocumented but remnants of their camps and villages are still found.

The Norseman, Erik the Red, explored and named Greenland from 982-985, after being outlawed for three years on account of manslaughter in Iceland. In 986, Erik led the first settlers from Iceland and by the year 1000 AD, some 3000 people had arrived from both Iceland and Scandinavia and gradually settled the southwest coast of Greenland from Cape Farewell to present-day Nuuk. This small community survived for 500 years. Why they finally disappeared is still a great mystery.

Around 1000 AD, Leif Eriksson, son of Erik the Red, led an expedition to areas in present-day Canada, naming these: Helluland, Markland and Vinland. A settlement has been excavated at L'Anse-aux-Meadows in Newfoundland. Thus, the Norseman is considered to be the first European ever to set foot on the North American mainland.

In seach of a northern sea route to the Orient

As the Osmanli, in the middle of the 15th century, blocked the old trade routes to the Orient, Europeans became determined to find a sea route to the Far East. The Portuguese were the first to find such a route, south of Africa. The southern sea routes were soon controlled by the Portuguese and the Spanish, therefore other marine nations like Great Britain and Holland started looking for an alternative, northern route to the Orient.

In the search for such a route, Giovanni Cabot (John Cabot) in 1497 discovered Labrador, Newfoundland and Nova Scotia. Martin Frobisher initiated the actual search for a northwest passage during his three journeys in 1576-78. In 1585-87 John Davis discovered the Davis Strait and followed the west coast of Greenland up to 72°12' N. Due to the geography of Greenland, the later European exploration of the remote northern parts happened step by step along two different routes, a westerly and an easterly.

The oldest written account of North and Northeast Greenland was given by the great English mariner Henry Hudson (1550-1611), who followed the east coast of Greenland northwards during his search for a north-eastern sea route to the Orient. On 21 June 1607 Hudson, onboard the *Hopewell*, wrote: "And considering wee knew no name given to this land, wee thought good to name it Hold-with-Hope, lying in 73 degrees of latitude (Asher 1860). Hold-with-Hope had been given its name, the oldest placename still in use in Northeast Greenland. In 1610 Hudson set out on a new attempt to find a route, this time west of Greenland. On this journey, in 1611, his crew mutinied and set Hudson, with his son and seven men, adrift in a small boat, without food or water. He was never seen again.

A few years after Hudson's attempts, William Baffin (c.1584-1622) on board *Discovery* under the command of Robert Bylot (who was formerly with Henry Hudson) explored the waters along the west coast. They reached 77°30' N and on the 16 July 1616 they discovered the entrance to Smith Sound, 'the greatest and largest sound in all this bay' as Baffin described it.

However, two hundred years were to elapse before a new expedition ventured into these northern regions. This was the British expedition in 1818 with *Hecla* and *Griper* under the leadership of John Ross and Edward Parry (1790-1855). Curiously enough Ross, on his chart, closed Smith Sund to the north, indicating it as a small bay.

Discovering the land behind the ice

Between 1600 and 1700, an enormous whaling industry developed along the edge of the northern icecap. Among the British whalers was William Scoresby Junior (1789-1857) who, in 1822, succeeded in entering open coastal water at 74°N with the vessels *Baffin* and *Fame* of Hull, outlining the eastern coastline southwards and finally exploring Scoresby Sund. William Scoresby Jr. is considered one of the founders of modern arctic exploration.

The following year, 1823, the British explorers Edward Sabine (1788-1883) and Douglas Charles Clavering (1794-1827) visited the area between Shannon Ø and Gael Hamke Bugt with their vessel *Griper*. In Gael Hamke Bugt, at Dødemandsbugten (Dead Mans Bay), an Inuit settlement was discovered, consisting of 12 persons, men, women and children. This is the only known encounter between Europeans and natives in Northeast Greenland.

The disappearance of Sir John Franklin and his men with the ships *Erebus* and *Terror* in 1845, during their search for the Northwest Passage, resulted in more than 40 rescue expeditions in the mid 19th century. Most of these went into the Canadian arctic, where traces of the Franklin expedition were found, but some also came into Greenland waters and resulted in a renewed interest in the Greenland arctic. One expedition was led by the British Royal Navy commander Edward Augustus Inglefield (1820-1894) who, with his ship *Isabel*, passed Kap Alexander on the west coast and, on 27 August 1852, reached 78°28' N. Inglefield thereby reopened Smith Sund, a discovery that had a large influence on later attempts to reach the North Pole.

The American physician and scientist Elisha Kent Kane (1820-1857), led the Second American Grinnell Expedition in the *Advance* from 1853-1855, through Smith Sound and into the basin now bearing his name, remaining there for 21 months. This expedition was the first to winter north of Smith Sound and explored as far as Kap Constitution at 80°35' N. When provisions ran low, Kane and his group abandoned the *Advance* and set out for the Danish settlements in West Greenland, reaching Upernavik in August 1855 after a hazardous overland journey of three months.

Dr. Isaac Israel Hayes (1832-1881), who had joined Kane's expedition as physician, led, in 1860, a new American expedition with the ship *United States*, the object being 'to complete the survey of the north coasts of Greenland and Grinnell Land, and to make such explorations as I might find practicable in the direction of the North Pole.' At his northernmost point, Hayes reached Cape Lieber on 18 May 1861 at 81°37' N on the east coast of Ellesmere Island. As to the results of the expedition, Hayes said: 'I have shown that open (Polar) sea exists.'

On the east coast of Greenland, the first real scientific expedition was the German Die Zweite Deutsche Nordpolarfahrt 1869-70, led by Captain Karl Koldewey (1837-1908). The plan was to survey the eastern coast of Greenland north of the 74th latitude. Two vessels, *Germania* and *Hansa*, were equipped for two years but near the coast of Greenland, *Hansa* was caught in the pack ice and shipwrecked. The crew miraculously reached West Greenland after 200 days of drifting on an ice floe. *Germania* reached the coast, where Koldewey led the vessel and her crew to a winter harbour at the south point of Sabine Ø. The expedition accomplished the preliminary mapping of the coast between 73° and 77° N.

Towards the North Pole and across the Inland Ice

An attempt to reach the North Pole along the Smith Sund route in 1871 was led by the American explorer Charles Francis Hall (1821-1871). On board *Polaris*, the expedition reached its northernmost point on 31 August 1871 at 82°26' N. Hall died under mysterious conditions during the wintering in Polaris Bay in 1871. As recently as 1968, it was established that Hall was murdered. He had been poisoned with arsenic.

A new North Pole expedition in 1875 was placed in the hands of one of the ablest men of the British Navy, Captain George Strong Nares (1831-1915). Two stoutly built steamers, the *Alert* and the *Discovery*, with an expedition totalling 120 members, were at his disposal. The expedition undertook a much needed re-mapping of the Greenland coast between Washington Land and Wullfs Land. In the spring of 1876 the expedition reached 83°20' N.

On the occasion of the first international polar year, 1882-83, the United States decided to establish a station north of the 81st latitude at, or near, Lady Franklin Bay where the *Discovery* had itís winter-quarters during Nare's expedition. In 1881 a military expedition under the command of Adolphus Washington Greely (1844-1935) was sent out with the ship *Proteus*. After unloading the expedition at Fort Conger, the *Proteus* returned southwards, but was crushed in the ice. The expedition reached 83°23' N 40°46' W on 13 May 1882. Unfortunately the expedition could not be relieved until 1884, by which time 19 out of the 25 members had died of starvation and scurvy.

Norwegian Fridthof Nansen (1861-1930), famous for his voyage across the Polar Sea with the *Fram* and later to become famous as a statesman and scientist, achieved the first crossing of the Greenland Icecap in 1888. He and his five companions completed the 600 km sledge journey in 36 days.

The American polar explorer Robert Edwin Peary (1856-1920) devoted 23 years of his life to polar exploration with the goal of being the first man to reach the North Pole. From 1886 to 1909 he led eight expeditions, all with more or less relevance to Greenland. Among his many achievements, in 1892 he made a journey across the inland ice to Navy Cliff, East Greenland, and back. In 1900 he made a journey around the north of Greenland to Kap Clarence Wyckoff. Peary was the first person to establish that Greenland is an island.

Completing the ring

In the years 1891-92, Carl Ryder led the Danish Den Østgrønlandske Ekspedition, which used the vessel *Hekla* for its survey of Scoresby Sund on the east coast where they wintered on Danmarks Ø.

In the summer of 1899 a Swedish expedition visited central Northeast Greenland. This expedition was led by Alfred Gabriel Nathorst (1850-1921) and used the ship *Antarctic*. Due to extremely favourable ice conditions, they succeeded during three hectic weeks in mapping the widely branched fjord complex between the 72nd and the 74th latitude; that is the area between Kong Oscar Fjord and Moskusoksefjord.

The Danish Carlsbergfondets Ekspedition til Østgrønland travelled in the summer of 1900, under command of Georg Carl Amdrup (1866-1947) on the ship *Antarctic*, to the area between Kong Oscar Fjord and Scoresby Sund.

The French duke Louis Philippe Robert d'Orléans (1869-1926) on the *Belgica* mapped, during the summer of 1905, the coast between about 77° and 79° N.

Finally, under the leadership of the Danish journalist and polar explorer Ludvig Mylius-Erichsen (1872-1907), the Danmark-ekspeditionen was sent out (in 1906) to survey the last unknown section of coastal Greenland. *Danmark*, the expedition vessel, was anchored in the vicinity of Kap Bismarck on the east coast and this place was given the name Danmark Havn. From here, the expedition carried out extensive travels in the following two years. In March 1907, four sledge teams were sent northwards. Unfortunately the expedition ended in tragedy as Mylius-Erichsen and the two other participants in his team perished during their attempt to return to the ship from North Greenland. Apart from this, the expedition was a major success and, on 12th May 1907, the team led by Lieutenant Johan Peter Koch (1870-1928) reached Peary's cairn at Kap Bridgman. The coast of Greenland had thus been travelled and mapped in its entire length. The ring was complete.

The Danmark-ekspeditionen marked the end of the initial mapping of Greenland. It also marked the beginning of a new era, where Denmark took over the leadership of, and responsibility for, the exploration of Greenland. More than 100 scientific expeditions from a number of countries have continued research in Northeast Greenland. These include large government-financed expeditions as well as smaller, private groups. It is not within the scope of this book to describe all of these expeditions, but it should be mentioned, that in the years 1926-39 and 1947-58, the Danish polar explorer and geologist Lauge Koch led the most extensive series of scientific expeditions to Northeast Greenland thus far. From 1929-58, he planned and led expeditions to the area almost every year, except during the second world war.

One of the latest initiatives is a permanent research station at Zackenberg. A research programme called ZERO (Zackenberg Ecological Research Operations) is attached to this station. ZERO is a Danish contribution to Global Change research, in order to establish a base line from which all future ecological changes can be evaluated.

Administration of North & Northeast Greenland

As long as Northeast Greenland had no commercial value, no one cared to whom it belonged. When this question finally had to be answered, it led to a dispute between Denmark and Norway. This took place between 1921 and 1933 and escalated into a conflict concerning the historical affiliation of Greenland.

Erik the Red, or Eirik Raude, in 986 led a Norse settlement in West Greenland, where two settlements, Østerbygden and Vesterbygden, were founded. In 1261 these areas were annexed in the Norgesvældet by the Norwegian king. As Norway and Denmark formed a united kingdom in 1380, this also included the Greenland settlements. From around 1350 AD, the supply traffic to Greenland declined and stopped altogether in the 15th century. The kingdom of Denmark-Norway resumed regular contact with Greenland in 1721, when Hans Egede founded the colony of Godthaab. By then the old Norse culture in Greenland had completely disappeared.

In 1776 all trade in Greenland was monopolised under Den Kongelige Grønlandske Handel (KGH or the Royal Greenland

Trading Company), and administered from Copenhagen. In 1814, as a consequence of the peace treaty of Kiel, the Danish-Norwegian kingdom was divided up. In the fourth article of the treaty, it was decided that: 'The Kingdom of Norway ... as well as the additional belongings (Greenland, Faeroe Islands and Iceland not included) must in the future belong to His Majesty the King of Sweden ...'

The contents of the inserted paragraph caused much disapproval and anger in Norway, but the Norwegians were occupied with other matters for the next century. At the end of the first world war, Greenland entered the arena again. It was now claimed that only the colonised areas in West Greenland and around Ammassalik in East Greenland were included under Danish sovereignty. The Danish government wanted to clarify this uncertainty and began to gather recognition from the states involved, that the whole of Greenland was included under Danish sovereignty. Recognition was obtained from USA in 1916, from France, Japan, Great Britain, and Italy in 1920, and from Sweden in 1921.

With Norway, the matter had been raised in 1919 during the peace conference following WW1. Norway wanted sovereignty over Svalbard, asked for Danish recognition of this, and received it. Denmark, in return, received an oral assurance from the Norwegian Minister of Foreign Affairs, concerning the question of Greenland. Denmark perceived this as a binding promise, and did not ask for a confirmation in writing until 1921. Norway hesitated, and the answer failed to come.

The East Greenland Agreement

Between 1919 and 1921, the Norwegian government changed its attitude towards the issue. It was realised that Norwegian fishermen had considerable economic interests in East Greenland, which could be jeopardised by an expanded Danish sovereignty. After a number of diplomatic contacts between the two countries, Norway claimed that the oral assurance had only been a preliminary and non-binding commitment. The Danes, however, chose to consider the statement as binding. Referring to this, Denmark issued a decree on 10 May 1921, announcing that the Danish administration now included the whole of Greenland. Norway refused to accept this and a strong anti-Danish feeling arose in Norway. From 1921, a movement grew in Norway, recommending an occupation of East Greenland.

In the autumn of 1923, delegations from the two countries met to negotiate an agreement. It immediately proved impossible to compromise on the issue of sovereignty. Consequently the agreement signed on 9 July 1924 only dealt with the practical regulations of the situation in East Greenland. The question of sovereignty was still unanswered. That agreement would stand for 20 years, but both Danes and Norwegians anticipated that the eighth article of the agreement would eventually be invoked. This article implied that any disagreement in interpreting the agreement was to be settled by The International Court of Justice in The Hague. Realising this, both countries tried, from 1924 to 1930, to strengthen their position through scientific and trapping activities in Northeast Greenland.

In 1930 the conflict sharpened. As the Norwegian government still refused the idea of occupying the territory, the Greenland movement within Norway arranged a private occupation. On 29 June 1931, the press in Norway announced that Hallvard Devold and four other trappers from Arktisk Næringsdrift, in the name of the Norwegian King, had occupied the area between Carlsberg Fjord and Bessel Fjord. On 27 June they hoisted their flag in Myggbukta, over what they named Erik Raude's Land.

On 10 July, the Norwegian government gave in to public pressure and confirmed by royal resolution that the area between 71°30' and 75°40' was now under Norwegian sovereignty. On 11 July, the Danish government summoned the dispute to the International Court of Justice in The Hague, claiming that the Norwegian occupation was unlawful and invalid.

On 5 April 1933 the court announced the verdict: East Greenland was to be placed under Danish sovereignty.

The Police Service, 1930-41

From 1930, Denmark and Norway had each appointed public officials in Northeast Greenland. As a consequence of the verdict in The Hague, the Norwegian mandate was annulled. However, along with the verdict, criticism was raised regarding Denmark's inadequate maintenance of sovereignty. Therefore, in 1934 the polar explorer Captain Ejnar Mikkelsen was appointed Inspector of the East Coast, subdued to Grønlands Styrelse (Administration of Greenland). In reality it was Lauge Koch and the station managers at Eskimonæs and Ella Ø, who practised the police duty until it was transferred to Nordøstgrønlands Slædepatrulje in 1941.

The agreement on Greenland's defence

From spring 1940, life in Northeast Greenland was overtaken by the war. Exploration stopped, trapping ceased gradually and the administration and supply service became subject to the vicissitudes of war.

When Germany occupied Denmark on 9 April 1940, not only the physical connections, such as supply services, between Denmark and Greenland were interrupted but the invisible ties of administration between Greenland and Denmark were also broken.

The Provincial Governors of North and South Greenland, Eske Brun and Axel Svane, established a unified administration in Godthaab (Nuuk) and thereafter governed Greenland on their own responsibility. Eske Brun became the actual leader in Greenland when Svane moved to the USA in the beginning of 1941, to become Greenland representative to the US administration.

With regard to supplies, Greenland was in a very difficult situation but managed to replace the supplies from Denmark with goods from the United States. The income from cryolite mining in Ivigtut in West Greenland served as payment. Cryolite also had a significant importance in the Greenland defence agreement, signed on 9 April 1941 in Washington D.C., between the United States and the Danish ambassador, Henrik Kauffmann. Cryolite was used to produce aluminium for the aviation industry. Ivigtut was the only place where natural cryolite was obtainable, and the supplies had a vital strategic importance for the American military industry. The mineral was so important that Great Britain and Canada discussed a Canadian occupation of Greenland to ensure the safety of the cryolite. This was unacceptable to the United States. Instead, it was agreed that the United States and Canada should defend Greenland as long as it was cut off from Denmark, while they in return received supplies of cryolite. The Americans were also permitted to establish air bases in Greenland. US Coast Guard vessels would patrol the coastal waters forming a squadron called The Greenland Patrol and The Greenland Naval Patrol.

The Weather Front, 1940-45

From 1941, West Greenland could be regarded as secured against German aggression. The situation was, however, different in Northeast Greenland where naval patrolling was possible only during the summer. Furthermore, the fighting here was not about a specific place or tangible assets; it was a war about weather reports; vitally important for military operations in the North Atlantic.

As early as summer 1940, German interests tried to establish a weather service via a Danish middleman. Four Danes were set ashore at Kap Biot where they started building a winter cabin. The cabin was finished on 7 September, but the allied naval vessel *Fridtjof Nansen* arrived the same day, the Danes and their equipment were taken on board and the new station was burnt down.

To Eske Brun and the Allies, it was obvious that Germany would soon try again to establish a weather service in Northeast Greenland: "In the summer of 1941, I made a deal with the American authorities that the administration (in Nuuk) should establish a sledge patrol service on this coast. The Americans should support it by means of transportation and bring supplies in the summer and deliver different equipment, but the service was entirely under the authority of the (Danish) administration. It was a sort of police duty where you should patrol the entire coast from Kap Dalton, a bit south of Scoresbysund, to Ile de France; one thousand km in a straight line." (Brun 1985). In the long run no activity could remain unobserved by people with local knowledge, who patrolled the hideouts by dog sledge in the winter.

It was the chief of The Greenland Patrol, commander Edward H. Smith, nick-named 'Iceberg Smith,' who took care of the practical implementation of Nordøstgrønlands Slædepatrulje in August 1941, and established three patrol districts: Eskimonæs, Ella Ø and Scoresbysund. In the summer of 1941, Smith was in charge of the three US Coast Guard cutters, *Northland*, *North Star* and *Bear*. They succeeded in hindering an attempt to establish a German-controlled weather station at Jonsbu.

The sledge patrol north of Scoresbysund consisted, in 1941-42, of nine Danes and one Norwegian. This small force was supplemented with two Greenlandic sledge drivers. The winter was undramatic, although some German aeroplanes were observed.

In 1942, the American naval patrol returned with supplies and orders to patrol the coast with *Northland* and *North Star*. However, the German weather ship *Sachsen* managed to reach Sabine Ø unnoticed at the end of August 1942. This German expedition of 18 men established their wintering quarters at Hansa Bugt, and from here they began regular transmissions of weather information. On 11th March 1943, men from Nordøstgrønlands Slædepatrulje became aware of the German presence. When discovered, the Germans attacked Eskimonæs on 23 March. The station was captured, but the inhabitants managed to escape. On their return to Hansa Bugt, Germans killed the Danish patrolman Eli Knudsen at Sandodden and captured the patrolmen Peter Nielsen and Marius Jensen. They soon let Peter Nielsen escape and, in May 1943, the German commander, Hermann Ritter, and Jensen turned up in Scoresbysund, with

Ritter now being the prisoner.

The Americans tried to bring the German weather service to an end. Under the command of Bernt Balchen, the US Army Air Corps bombed Eskimonæs on 13th May 1943 and the Hansa Bugt base on 25 May. These air strikes did not, however, stop the German weather reporting.

A command force from *Northland* attacked the base at Sabine Ø on 21 July 1943. The Germans had already been evacuated by seaplane one month earlier, leaving behind one man, Rudolf Sensse, who had missed the evacuation. Like Hermann Ritter, the Americans took him prisoner of war.

To replace the destroyed headquarters at Eskimonæs, a new station, Dødemandsbugten, was established in 1943. The USCG vessels *Northland* and *North Star* patrolled the coast.

In November 1943, the sledge patrol revealed a new German landing, this time at Kap Sussi on Shannon Ø. On 22 April 1944, Danes attacked the German camp. The German military leader, Gerhard Zacher, was the only one killed during the fight. The Danes, however, had to retreat and the Germans continued their weather service unobstructed until they were evacuated by plane in June 1944.

The sledge patrol moved from Dødemandsbugten to their new headquarters at Daneborg. Niels Ove Jensen led the patrol, which in 1944-45 consisted of six Danes and two or three Greenlanders.

In 1944, the USCG vessels *Northland, Southwind, Eastwind, Evergreen* and *Storis* participated in the patrolling. On 1 September 1944, *Northland* attacked and sank the German ship *Kehdingen* off Store Koldewey and took the crew prisoners. On 4 October, a landing party from *Eastwind* captured eleven Germans from operation Edelweiss II at Tyskerdepotet on Lille Koldewey. This was the last act of war in Northeast Greenland.

The postwar period

After the second world war, exploration and commercial business were resumed. The State of Denmark had two important tasks:

to ensure continuous sovereignty and to obtain regular weather information. Shortly after the war, a number of new stations were built in order to accommodate these tasks.

At the end of the war, Grønlands Radio-og Vejrtjeneste immediately began to re-organise the weather service in Greenland, to cope with the requirements of fast-growing intercontinental air traffic. In 1947, the Daneborg Vejrstation was enlarged. Until its final closure in 1975, the station had a yearly crew of around seven employees.

In 1948 a radiosonde-operated weather station, Danmarkshavn Vejrstation, was established. Manned by ten to twelve employees, it is still in service as an important station in the international weather service.

In 1952-53, Station Nord was established for the USA as a weather station and an emergency airfield for the Thule Air Base.

The Sledge Patrol

Nordøstgrønlands Slædepatrulje was dissolved on the German capitulation in 1945. The police authority north of Scoresbysund was transferred to station managers at the weather stations Daneborg and Danmarkshavn. However, the escalation of the cold war soon led to a demand for a systematic surveillance of North and Northeast Greenland.

In 1950 a military sledge patrol was formed in great secrecy under the code-name Operation Resolut. For the first year, the patrol was based at Ella Ø, but in 1951 it moved to Daneborg where a new headquarters, Sirius Daneborg, was established. In 1953 the patrol changed its name to Sirius, named after the brightest star in the constellation of Canis Major and it was under this name that the patrol eventually became known to the public.

The task of Slædepatruljen Sirius is surveillance of the uninhabited area between Liverpool Land on the east coast and Nares Strait on the north coast, a straight-line distance of around 2,100 km. The patrolling is carried out by dog sledge in the winter and patrol boats in the summer. The patrol is responsible for maintaining sovereignty over this vast area and it also exercises the civilian police authority in the area. The crew, consisting of twelve men, are all officers or non-commissioned officers, who volunteer for a two-year period of service. A sledge team, two men and eleven Greenlandic sledge dogs, can be on continuous patrol for four to five months. Of the 250 or more men who have served with the patrol since 1950, only one has perished during service. To date, Sirius has travelled more than 700,000 km patrolling the coast of North and Northeast Greenland.

The National Park

The vision of establishing a national park in the uninhabited area of North and Northeast Greenland, matured in the 1960's. The idea was to create a refuge for wildlife and a biological 'bank' from which the 'interest' would accrue to the neighbouring Greenlandic communities of Illoqqortoormiit (Scoresbysund) and Avanersuaq (Thule).

This idea was realised in 1974 when the largest national park in the world became a fact. Following an extension in 1988, the Nationalparken Nord-og Østgrønland today covers 972,000 square km, of which much is inland ice. Anyone who wishes to visit the national park must apply for a permit. The National Park has resulted in total protection, not only of animal life, but also for archaeological items, plants and trapping cabins with their contents of antiquities.

B. RELATED READING

Balchen, B, Ford, C, & Lafarge, O. (1944) *War Below Zero.* Houghton Mifflin, Cambridge, Mass.

Banks, M. (1975) *Greenland.* J. M. Dent, London,

Freuchen, P. (1936) *Arctic Adventure.* Heinnemann, London.

Howarth, D. (1957) *The Sledge Patrol.* Collins, London.

Koch, L. (1955) Report on the expeditions to Central East Greenland, 1926-1939. *Medd. Grønland*, 143 [2].

Lindsay, M. (1935) *Sledge.* Cassell, London.

Mikkelsen, E. (1913) *Lost in the Arctic.* Heinnemann, London & New York.

Mikkelsen, P. S. (2000) *Sirius gennem 50 år.* Gyldendal, København.

Mikkelsen, P. S. (1994) *Nordøst-Grønland 1908-60, fangstmandsperioden.* Gyldendal, København.

Mylius-Erichsen, L. & Moltke, H. (1906) *Grønland.* Copenhagen & Kristiania.

Simpson, C. J. W. (1957) *North Ice.* Hodder & Stoughton, London.

Staib, B. *(1963) Across Greenland in Nansen's Track.* George Allen & Unwin, London.

Woolley, S. (2004) *Greenland Ventures.* Athena Press, Twickenham.

C. TRANSLATOR'S NOTES

Explanations or translations of Danish preserved in the text are shown in brackets by the translator.

Place names have been left in the original Danish in order to retain compatibility with maps of Greenland. Some translations are given in the text and a summary of useful geographical terms is presented below. There are some differences in Danish spelling between new and old versions, both here and on maps. For instance, ø can be replaced by oe, å by aa, and æ by ae in both upper and lower case.

Some of the Danish nicknames in the original Danish text do not translate and have been replaced by an English word or phrase, for example 'fup' the nickname for a member of the Sirius Patrol, has been replaced by 'Sirius man'.

Bjerg	Mountain	*Hav*	Sea/Ocean
Sø	Lake	*Hus*	House
Bre	Glacier	*Hytte*	Hut
Ø (en)	Island (the)	*Is*	Ice
Øvre	Upper	*Kap*	Cape
Bugt	Bay	*Sund*	Sound
Dal	Valley	*Stor*	Great
Elv	River	*Storis*	literally, Great Ice
Fjeld	Mountain	*Vejr*	Weather
Kap	Cape		

D. SLEDGE AND TENT DESIGNS

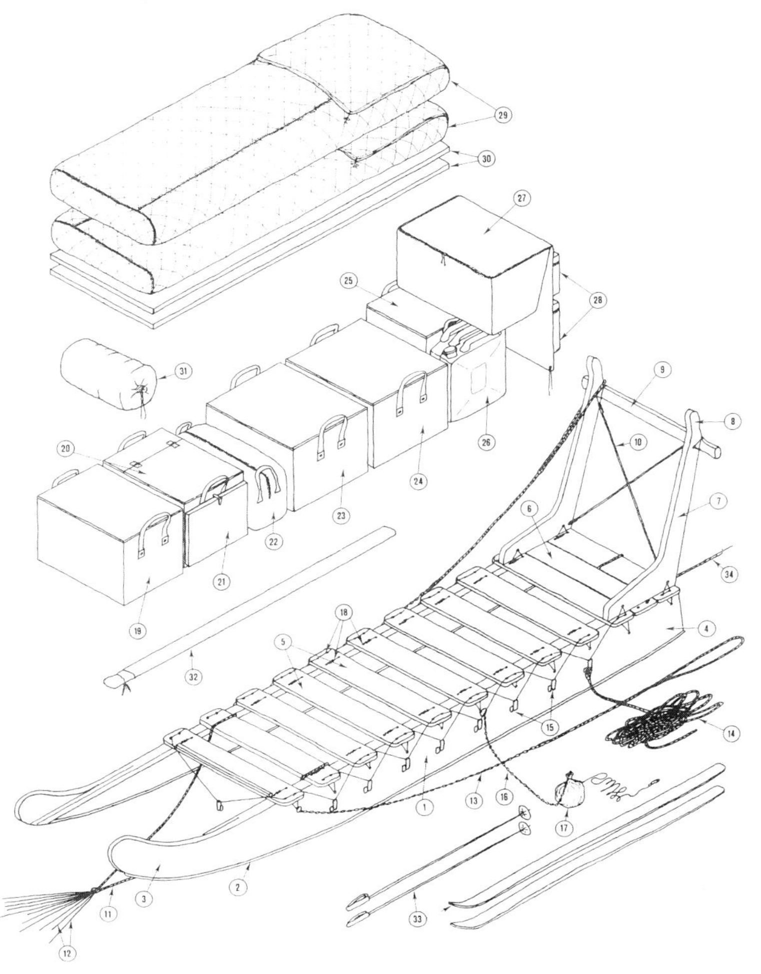

D. SIRIUS SLEDGE WITH TRAVELLING EQUIPMENT (IDEALISED)

1. *Sledge runner*
2. *Steel surface on runner*
3. *Upswing*
4. *Heel*
5. *Bottom boards*
6. *Spare bottom board*
7. *Upright*
8. *Handlebar*
9. *Crosspiece*
10. *Handlebar brace wires*
11. *Sledge trace*
12. *Dog traces*
13. *Steering/braking line*
14. *Load lash line*
15. *Lashing hooks*
16. *Brake chain*
17. *Brake chain bag*
18. *Construction lashings*
19. *Radio box*
20. *Food box*
21. *Board for saucepans*
22. *Dog food bag*
23. *Primus box*
24. *Clothes box*
25. *Sledge box*
26. *Jerrycan for paraffin*
27. *Sledge bag*
28. *Pockets*
29. *Sleeping bags*
30. *Groundsheet*
31. *Tent*
32. *Tent poles in bag*
33. *Spare skis and sticks*
34. *Drag rope*

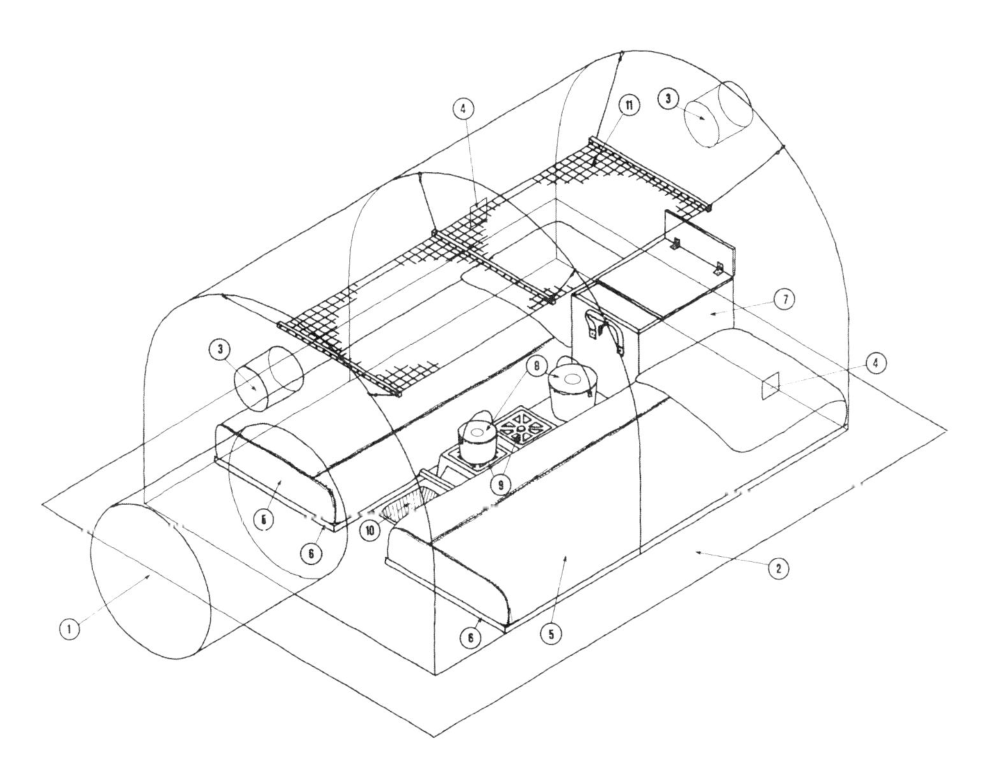

SIRIUS TENT AND CONTENTS (IDEALISED)

1. *Sleeve (tunnel) door*
2. *Snow valence*
3. *Ventilators*
4. *Windows*
5. *Sleeping bags*
6. *Groundsheet*
7. *Food box*
8. *Cooking pots*
9. *Primus stoves*
10. *Rubbish hole*
11. *Tent nets*